A THEOLOGY OF Q

A THEOLOGY
OF Q

Eschatology, Prophecy, and Wisdom

Richard A. Edwards

FORTRESS PRESS
Philadelphia

Dedicated to the memory of my father
Francis Reed Edwards

CONTENTS

PREFACE

This book is intended to be both a new interpretation of the Q source and a text useful in college and seminary classrooms. To satisfy both demands, the text of Matthew and/or Luke is printed at many points to assist the reader in following the discussion.

The exact text of the Q source is, of course, unrecoverable. Almost every suggested reconstruction of the text is different from any other to a greater or lesser degree, because each scholar has attributed to Q material which is found *only* in Matthew or Luke. The assumption behind this procedure states that the influence of Q can be recognized in the pericope and that the other evangelist has deleted the material; even though such a passage does not fit the normal definition for Q (found in Matthew and Luke but not in Mark), it still deserves inclusion.

It is because of this problem that the following "Guide" does not attempt to give a precise verbal definition of Q. The parallel passages of Matthew and Luke are noted in their entirety and the reader is encouraged to make his own judgments about the extent of the text. In certain instances, Mark is also included when there is a possibility of interaction between the two traditions. Again, the reader is requested to check the evidence on his own.

I wish to acknowledge the assistance and support of Norman Perrin of the University of Chicago. It was under his guidance that the first elements of this argument were developed and he has encouraged and criticized it as it has evolved. Much of the preliminary work was done with the help of a Research and Creativity

Grant from the Board of College Education and Church Vocations of the Lutheran Church in America, for which I am grateful. My thanks also to Judy and Tom McKee who, as student assistants at Thiel College, helped in establishing some of the basic groundwork; to Nancy Chapman, Charlotte Scarborough, and Mary Bowman for their patience and skill in typing numerous versions of the manuscript; and to Mary Bowman and Dabney Whipple for their help in preparing the indexes. Finally, I wish to thank the College of Arts and Sciences at Virginia Tech for research funds in support of the computer studies which helped to develop my understanding of the material. Part of that work is now available from The Scholars Press under the title *A Concordance to Q*.

Blacksburg, Virginia   RAE
July 1975

GUIDE TO THE
CONTENTS OF Q

NUMBER	TITLE	MATTHEW	MARK	LUKE
13	Commissioning of 70	9:37–38		10:1–12
		10:7–16		
14	Woes on Galilee	11:20–24		10:13–15
				10:12
15	Whoever Hears You, Hears Me	10:40		10:16
16	Thanksgiving and Blessedness of Disciples	11:25–27		10:21–24
		13:16–17		
17	Lord's Prayer	6:9–13		11:1–4
18	Encouragement to Pray	7:7–11		11:9–13
19	Beelzebul Controversy	12:22–30	3:22–27	11:14–23
		9:32–34		
20	Return of the Evil Spirit	12:43–45		11:24–26
21	Sign of Jonah	12:38–42	8:11–12	11:16
		16:1–4		11:29–32
22	Sound Eye	6:22–23		11:34–36
23	Against the Pharisees	23:4–36	7:1–9	11:37–54
24	Fearless Confession	10:26–33		12:2–9
25	Sin against the Holy Spirit	12:31–32	3:29–30	12:10
26	Assistance of the Holy Spirit	10:19–20	13:11	12:11–12
				21:14–15
27	Anxiety	6:25–34		12:22–32
28	Treasures in Heaven	6:19–21		12:33–34
29	Watchfulness and Faithfulness	24:42–51		12:35–48
30	Divisions in Households	10:34–36		12:49–53
31	Signs of the Times	16:2–3		12:54–56
32	Agreement with Accuser	5:25–26		12:57–59
33	Mustard Seed	13:31–32	4:30–32	13:18–19
34	Leaven	13:33		13:20–21
35	Exclusion from the Kingdom	7:13–14		13:22–30
		7:22–23		
		8:11–12		
		19:30		

NUMBER	TITLE	MATTHEW	MARK	LUKE
36	Lament over Jerusalem	23:37–39		13:34–35
37	Great Supper	22:1–14		14:15–24
38	Conditions of Discipleship	10:37–38		14:25–33
39	Parable of Salt	5:13	9:49–50	14:34–35
40	Lost Sheep	18:12–14		15:1–7
41	Two Masters	6:24		16:13
42	Concerning the Law	11:12–13 5:18		16:16–17
43	Warning against Offenses	18:6–7	9:42	17:1–3a
44	On Forgiveness	18:15 18:21–22		17:3b–4
45	On Faith	17:19–20	9:28–29	17:5–6
46	Day of the Son of Man	24:23 24:26–27 24:37–39 24:17–18 10:39 24:40–41 24:28	13:19–23 13:14–16	17:22–37
47	Parable of Pounds	25:14–30		19:11–27
48	Precedence	19:28	10:41–45	22:28–30

I

INTRODUCTION

Mystery seems always to grasp our attention. When students suspect that there is a mysterious "document" which has never been found or fully explained (despite the huge amounts of time and energy which have been expended in the study of the Gospels) there is often a heightened interest and skepticism about the details of such an hypothesis. Although the discovery of the Dead Sea Scrolls does not shed any direct, immediate light on the problem of Q, the spectacular nature of the find has created an interest in other mysteries, particularly missing "documents," from the early days of Christianity. This general context was probably the origin of a spy-style novel called *The Q Document* which appeared in 1964, speculating (wildly) about the consequences of the discovery of the original manuscript.[1]

Some of the uncertainty and confusion about Q can now be corrected. The development of redaction criticism, a method of inquiry into the interests and origins of gospel material, offers an approach which holds much promise. Redaction criticism is the label given to a specific method of inquiry which seeks to uncover the work of the final editor (redactor) who produced the document under examination. In many ways an extension of form criticism, this approach will be used in the major portions of this book to present a possible explanation of the specific material in Q. However, before a solution can be proposed, the problem must be fully explored.

1. James Hall Roberts, *The Q Document* (Greenwich, Conn.: Fawcett Publications, 1964).

1

The Q hypothesis is the result of the work of the source critics—the first stage in the historical-critical analysis of the Gospels. The advent of form criticism did not advance the discussion of Q but it did establish the context in which redaction criticism could pick up the clues laid bare by form analysis and offer us the chance to propose a solution. Thus, a review of the problem of Q as the background for the solution to be proposed here requires a clarification of the succession of methods used in the study of the Gospels and hopefully will lead to a healthy self-consciousness about the limits of this study as well.

THE SYNOPTIC PROBLEM

The classic solution to the interrelation of the first three Gospels —the two-source hypothesis—argues that Mark and a second source called Q (an abbreviation for the German word for source: *Quelle*)[2] were both used by Matthew and Luke in the writing of their Gospels. Based primarily on a literary analysis of similarities and differences among the three Synoptic Gospels, the two-source hypothesis is accepted as a starting point for the majority of those scholars working with the Gospel material.[3] In the following diagram M and L stand for the material that is found only in Matthew or Luke.

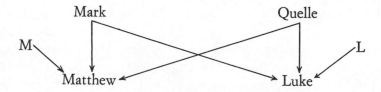

A synopsis of the Gospels is an indispensable tool and should be used in conjunction with any gospel analysis. All relevant passages

---

2. A. Robinson is reported to have claimed that he was the first to use the symbol Q for this source, because it followed "P" in the alphabet, his designation for Mark (the reminiscences of St. Peter). See Stephen Neill, *The Interpretation of the New Testament, 1861–1961* (New York: Oxford University Press, 1966), note 2 on p. 119.
3. The best description of this problem is contained in W. G. Kümmel, *Introduction to the New Testament* (Nashville: Abingdon Press, 1966), pp. 33–59. A historical treatment of the problem is now available in Kümmel's, *The New Testament: The History of the Investigation of Its Problem* (Nashville: Abingdon Press, 1972).

of Q are printed in synopsis form in Chapter VI.[4] This book assumes that the reader has a basic understanding of the methods and results of source criticism.

There are a few contemporary scholars who have challenged the two-source hypothesis for a variety of reasons. They argue that the evidence does not support the priority of Mark and, as a consequence, does not support, in any way, the hypothesis of Q, the second source. To date, however, very few gospel scholars have been convinced to abandon the classic solution; the majority continue to work with the assumption and results of the two-source hypothesis.[5]

The Q material was judged of secondary importance to Mark, primarily because it lacked narrative material. It was thought to be a supplement to the basic historical *kerygma*. Although the distinction between *kerygma* (proclamation) and *didache* (teaching) has been seriously questioned lately, it was at that time a very crucial factor in an evaluation of Q. Because the six-point *kerygma*, as outlined by Dodd[6] appeared to be a basic, primitive pattern, any source which did not contain this message was considered of secondary importance, i.e., as *didache*. Thus Q, designated "teaching," was a necessary supplement to the *kerygma*. During the era of the "Markan Hypothesis," approximately 1860–1950, attention was riveted to the primary source, Mark, while Q was merely a supplement used to fill out the Markan outline of the life of Jesus.

The change of interest which fostered a new concern for Q will be detailed in the next chapter. Before we can proceed with any analysis of Q, however, we must be able to agree on its limits, on what precisely is or is not Q material. There have been many attempts to reconstruct Q. In 1918 James Moffatt listed sixteen reconstructions,

---

4. The most complete and useful synopsis is the Greek edition of Kurt Aland, ed., *Synopsis Quattuor Evangeliorum* (Stuttgart: Württembergische Bibelanstalt, 1964), which is also available in a Greek-English edition with the RSV translation on facing pages.
5. William Farmer, *The Synoptic Problem* (New York: Macmillan, 1964) presents the most complete argument against Q. See also D. L. Dungan, "Mark—The Abridgment of Matthew and Luke" in *Jesus and Man's Hope,* vol. 1 (Pittsburgh: Pittsburgh Theological Seminary, 1970), pp. 50–97. Joseph Fitzmyer presents a typical response from the point of view of those who support the two-source hypothesis in the same volume, pp. 131–170.
6. C. H. Dodd, *The Apostolic Preaching and Its Development* (London: Hodder and Stoughton, 1936).

none of which were exactly alike.[7] Why should such a variety of opinions exist? It would seem that it is a rather straightforward decision: when Matthew and Luke agree against Mark, we have Q. Because this definition of Q is an important issue, some examples of the varieties of Q material are presented before a judgment is made.

#36 LAMENT OVER JERUSALEM

Mt. 23:37–39

(37) "O Jerusalem, Jerusalem, killing the prophets and stoning those who are sent to you! How often would I have gathered your children together as a hen gathers her brood under her wings, and you would not! (38) Behold, your house is forsaken and desolate. (39) For I tell you, you will not see me again, until you say, 'Blessed is he who comes in the name of the Lord.' "

Lk. 13:34–35

(34) "O Jerusalem, Jerusalem, killing the prophets and stoning those who are sent to you! How often would I have gathered your children together as a hen gathers her brood under her wings, and you would not! (35) Behold, your house is forsaken. And I tell you, you will not see me until you say, 'Blessed be he who comes in the name of the Lord.' "

In this saying we have a clear-cut case of almost precise verbal agreement. The slight differences that do occur do not affect the meaning but could be understood to be stylistic changes which each evangelist employed, either consciously or unconsciously. Such complete, precise agreement could not be explained in any other way, says the source critic, than to assume that Matthew and Luke have a second source in front of them which they are copying.

#14 WOES ON GALILEE

Mt. 11:20–24

(20) Then he began to upbraid the cities where most of his mighty works had been done, because they did not repent. (21) "Woe to you, Chorazin! woe to you, Bethsaida! for if the mighty works done in you had been done in Tyre and Sidon, they would have repented long ago in sackcloth and ashes. (22) But I tell you, it shall be more tolerable on the day of judgment for

Lk. 10:12–15

(12) "I tell you, it shall be more tolerable on that day for Sodom than for that town."

(13) "Woe to you, Chorazin! woe to you, Bethsaida! for if the mighty works done in you had been done in Tyre and Sidon, they would have repented long ago, sitting in sackcloth and ashes. (14) But it shall be more tolerable in the judgment for Tyre and

---

7. James Moffatt, *An Introduction to the Literature of the New Testament,* 3d rev. ed. (Edinburgh: T. & T. Clark, 1961 [1918]), pp. 194–206.

Tyre and Sidon than for you. (23)
And you, Capernaum, will you be
exalted to heaven? You shall be brought
down to Hades. For if the mighty works
done in you had been done in Sodom,
it would have remained until this day.
(24) But I tell you that it shall be
more tolerable on the day of judgment
for the land of Sodom than for you."

Sidon than for you. (15) And you,
Capernaum, will you be exalted to
heaven? You shall be brought to Hades."

The problem has become more complex. We now must decide
what to do with the material which is obviously a part of the pericope (paragraph or self-contained unit) but is not found in one of
the Gospels. Mt. 11:20 could be considered Matthew's addition, or
we could argue that Luke has deleted an introductory sentence which
he felt was superfluous. The same problem exists with the second
half of Mt. 11:23: is it Matthew's *addition* or did Luke *delete* it
from Q?

Secondly, we have a problem of arrangement or order within the
pericope. Mt. 11:24 is very similar to Lk. 10:12; Matthew uses it
as a conclusion, Luke as an introduction. It is definitely a Q saying
(Matthew = Luke [−Mark]). Has the change in placement (whether
it is the work of Matthew or Luke) caused a change in its precise
wording? An introduction turned into a conclusion (or vice versa)
may require rewriting.

#3 BEATITUDES

Mt. 5:3–12
(3) "Blessed are the poor in spirit,
for theirs is the kingdom of heaven.
(4) "Blessed are those who mourn,
for they shall be comforted.
(5) "Blessed are the meek, for they
shall inherit the earth.
(6) "Blessed are those who hunger and
thirst for righteousness, for they shall
be satisfied.
(7) "Blessed are the merciful, for
they shall obtain mercy.
(8) "Blessed are the pure in heart,
for they shall see God.
(9) "Blessed are the peacemakers,
for they shall be called sons of God.

Lk. 6:20b–23
(20b) "Blessed are you poor, for yours
is the kingdom of God.
(21) "Blessed are you that hunger
now, for you shall be satisfied.
"Blessed are you that weep now, for
you shall laugh.
(22) "Blessed are you when men
hate you, and when they exclude you
and revile you, and cast out your name
as evil, on account of the Son of
man! (23) Rejoice in that day, and
leap for joy, for behold, your reward is
great in heaven; for so their fathers
did to the prophets.

(10) "Blessed are those who are persecuted for righteousness' sake, for theirs is the kingdom of heaven.

(11) "Blessed are you when men revile you and persecute you and utter all kinds of evil against you falsely on my account.

(12) Rejoice and be glad, for your reward is great in heaven, for so men persecuted the prohphets who were before you."

The question here is not only with the variations *within* the final beatitude, but with whole sentences which could be integral to the material but which are found in Matthew and not in Luke. Has Matthew expanded or Luke deleted? On what basis can either conclusion be argued? Obviously, we are dealing with more than stylistic variations or corrections. Can the definition of Q be expanded to include some material found only in Matthew *or* Luke? On what basis can such a judgment be made?

#21 SIGN OF JONAH

Mt. 12:38–42

(38) Then some of the scribes and Pharisees said to him, "Teacher, we wish to see a sign from you."
(39) But he answered them, "An evil and adulterous generation seeks for a sign; but no sign shall be given to it except the sign of the prophet Jonah.
(40) For as Jonah was three days and three nights in the belly of the whale, so will the Son of man be three days and three nights in the heart of the earth.
(41) The men of Nineveh will arise at the judgment with this generation and condemn it; for they re-

Mk. 8:11–12

(11) The Pharisees came and began to argue with him, seeking from him a sign from heaven, to test him. (12) And he sighed deeply in his spirit, and said, "Why does this generation seek a sign? Truly, I say to you, no sign shall be given to this generation."

Lk. 11:16

(16) While others, to test him, sought from him a sign from heaven.

Lk. 11:29–32

(29) When the crowds were increasing, he began to say, "This generation is an evil generation; it seeks a sign, but no sign shall be given to it except the sign of Jonah. (30) For as Jonah became a sign to the men of Nineveh, so will the Son of man be to this generation. (31) The queen of the South will arise at the judgment with the men of this generation and condemn them; for she came from

pented at the preaching of Jonah and behold, something greater than Jonah is here. (42) The queen of the South will arise at the judgment with this generation and condemn it; for she came from the ends of the earth to hear the wisdom of Solomon and behold, something greater than Solomon is here."

the ends of the earth to hear the wisdom of Solomon, and behold, something greater than Solomon is here. (32) The men of Nineveh will arise at the judgment with this generation and condemn it; for they repented at the preaching of Jonah, and behold, something greater than Jonah is here."

Mt. 16:1–4

(1) And the Pharisees and Sadducees came, and to test him they asked him to show them a sign from heaven. (2) He answered them, "When it is evening, you say, 'It will be fair weather; for the sky is red.' (3) And in the morning, it will be stormy today, for the sky is red and threatening.' You know how to interpret the appearance of the sky, but you cannot interpret the signs of the times. (4) An evil and adulterous generation seeks for a sign, but no sign shall be given to it except the sign of Jonah." So he left them and departed.

The new factor here, of course, is the relation of Q to Mark. When we find Matthew and Luke agreeing because they are following Mark and then also when they are "following" Q, new problems arise. Is it possible that Mark has deleted an old tradition? Or is there a common tradition which is so widespread that it appears in two different sources and in modified forms? The problem of the relation of Mark and Q we will find later on to be of particular help in the attempt to identify the specific theological position of the Q community.

#37 GREAT SUPPER

Mt. 22:1–14

(1) And again Jesus spoke to them in parables, saying (2) "The kingdom of heaven may be compared to a king who gave a marriage feast for his son, (3) and sent his servants to call those who were invited to the marriage feast; but they would not come. (4) Again he sent other servants, saying, 'Tell those who are invited, Behold, I have made ready my dinner, my oxen and my fat calves are killed, and everything is ready; come to the marriage feast.' (5) But they made light of it and went off, one to his farm, another to his business, (6) while the rest seized his servants, treated them shamefully, and killed them. (7) The king was angry, and he sent his troops and destroyed those murderers and burned their city. (8) Then he said to his servants, 'The wedding is ready, but those invited were not worthy. (9) Go therefore to the thoroughfares, and invite to the marriage feast as many as you find.' (10) And those servants went out into the streets and gathered all whom they found, both bad and good; so the wedding hall was filled with guests.

(11) "But when the king came in to look at the guests, he saw there a man who had no wedding garment; (12) and he said to him, 'Friend, how did you get in here without a wedding garment?' And he was speechless. (13) Then the king said to the attendants, 'Bind him hand and foot, and cast him into the outer darkness; there men will weep and gnash their teeth.' (14) For many are called, but few are chosen."

Lk. 14:15–24

(15) When one of those who sat at table with him heard this, he said to him, "Blessed is he who shall eat bread in the kingdom of God!" (16) But he said to him, " A man once gave a great banquet, and invited many; (17) and at the time for the banquet he sent his servant to say to those who had been invited, 'Come; for all is now ready.' (18) But they all alike began to make excuses. The first said to him, 'I have bought a field, and I must go out and see it; I pray you, have me excused.' (19) And another said, 'I have bought five yoke of oxen, and I go to examine them; I pray you have me excused.' (20) And another said, 'I have married a wife, and therefore I cannot come.' (21) So the servant came and reported this to his master. Then the householder in anger said to his servant, 'Go out quickly to the streets and lanes of the city, and bring in the poor and maimed and blind and lame.' (22) And the servant said, 'Sir, what you commanded has been done, and still there is room.' (23) And the master said to the servant, 'Go out to the highways and hedges, and compel people to come in, that my house may be filled. (24) For I tell you, none of these men who were invited shall taste my banquet.' "

There can be little doubt that these two items stem from a common story. But the verbal similarity is very small. Jeremias and others have argued that a great deal of reworking has taken place as the church (at various stages) adapted the story to its changing interests.[8] For example, Luke's interest in the world-wide mission of Christianity is explicitly stated in the reference to the householder's order to go outside the city (Judaism) into the highways and hedges (Lk. 14:23). What then do we consider Q to be?

The working hypothesis for this study is that we cannot reconstruct Q beyond the verbal evidence. When Matthew and Luke agree exactly (with no dependence on Mark), that is Q. When the agreement is one of subject matter, we can recognize the influence of Q material but we cannot use such material to reconstruct the thought of Q. It may be possible once we have a firm understanding of the "precise Q" to suggest which evangelist has apparently preserved a more Q-like vocabulary or concept, *but* that can only be provisional, must be strictly limited, and should be noted as a possibility only.

It is for this reason, also, that there is no consideration here of manuscript variants, i.e., the problem of the text. The decision to adopt a manuscript reading which is not normally acceptable (using the United Bible Society text as a basis) would have to be argued on the grounds of the text-critical principle called the more difficult reading. However, such a decision could only be reached, aside from the grammatical considerations which the editors of the text have already weighed, by way of a clear grasp of the theological interests of the manuscript. This task still lies before us. Secondly, the problem is further intensified by the fact that Matthew and Luke have edited the material to incorporate it into their Gospels. If the student is interested in this aspect of the study of Q, there are a number of books which take up this problem in detail as well as the basic issues of text criticism.[9]

Part of the reason for this narrow definition of Q is the status of Q generally; it is, first of all, a hypothesis and the piling of hypothesis

---

8. Joachim Jeremias, *The Parables of Jesus,* rev. ed. (New York: Charles Scribner's Sons, 1963), pp. 63–66. Cf. also Norman Perrin, *Rediscovering the Teaching of Jesus* (New York: Harper & Row, 1967), pp. 110–114.

9. Paul Hoffmann, *Studien zur Theologie der Logienquelle,* NTAbh, n.f., 8 (Münster: Aschendorff, 1972); Paul D. Meyer, "The Community of Q" (Ph.D. dissertation, University of Iowa, 1967); Ronald D. Worden, "A Philological Analysis of Luke 6:20b–49 and Parallels" (Ph.D. dissertation, Princeton Seminary, 1973).

upon hypothesis is foolish. If the Q hypothesis is a realistic one, and if the Q material does reflect a consistent point of view from an early Christian community, the argument must be based on the hard evidence at hand. The reader will be able to appreciate this approach as we move into the discussion in subsequent chapters.

THE CONTENTS OF Q

The list of pericopes at the front of the book includes only those that contain Q material. The order of the material is based on the order of Q in Luke. It has often been argued that Q could not have existed as a document because Matthew and Luke do not agree in the arrangement of this common material—as they agree in following the order of events in Mark. However, if Q is primarily a collection of sayings, each evangelist could have adopted Mark's outline of the life of Jesus and then proceeded to insert the unordered Q material where it seemed most appropriate to him. Of special importance here is Vincent Taylor's article on the order of Q in which he shows that Luke's arrangement is usually followed by Matthew *if* we look independently at each of Matthew's five collections of sayings material.[10]

Although this should not be considered a final answer, it is enough to suggest that Luke may be closer to the original order of Q to permit the listing of contents in this way. This problem will be discussed later. It is not possible to construct a theology of Q on the basis of the order of the material and thus the arrangement of the contents is provisional.

The last decade has seen a renewed interest in Q which shows every sign of increasing. Why has it taken scholars one hundred years, since the acceptance of the two-source hypothesis, to concentrate their interest on such an important part of the synoptic material?

The primary reason is that their attention was focused on Mark. Mark is a document which was readily available and did not require reconstruction. But more importantly, both Matthew and Luke demonstrate how important Mark is to them not only by using much of his material but by also maintaining the basic Markan outline. We

10. Vincent Taylor, "The Original Order of Q," *New Testament Essays: Studies in Memory of T. W. Manson,* ed. A. J. Higgins (Manchester: University of Manchester Press, 1959), pp. 246–69.

must remember that during most of this time the writing of a life of Jesus was especially important to New Testament scholars. They were seeking a way of cutting through the church tradition (dogmatic influence) to find the real, historical Jesus. Source criticism gave them the basis for writing a life of Jesus, i.e., the Gospel according to Mark, a book available in specific form *and* a recognized authority (because Mark was used so carefully by Matthew and Luke).

With this focus on Mark, Q was neglected because it was hypothetical and unstructured. It was of secondary importance to Matthew and Luke and therefore ought to be so considered by the critics. But there was another reason for a delayed interest in Q. The content of Q is almost entirely sayings of Jesus. The source critics assumed that a collection of sayings would serve as an ethical guidebook for those who were members of the church. The tacit assumption is that the primary task of the early church was the missionary task. Thus Q can be explained as a later development, when new members of the community sought more information about the content of a Christian life. Q is *didache* and not *kerygma*, they assumed, secondary and thus less important. The following quote from Moffatt is typical of the source critic's evaluation:

> It [Q] is not a heterogeneous mass of logia, but a collection moulded by catechetical and homiletical processes, with sayings on the Kingdom grouped together for the purposes of edification and apologetic, strongly marked by eschatological traits, and shaped, more than once, by polemical interests. The outstanding features are the grouping of the sayings (which is not simply the work of Matthew's editor) and the emphatically Jewish Christian cast of some sections.[11]

The times have changed. Although source critics "discovered" Q, they did not foster any elaborate analysis of the material. It is only when form and redaction criticism raised questions about the possible origins of such material that the search for the theology of Q really became a matter of interest and importance.

---

11. Moffatt, *Introduction,* p.197.

APPROACHES TO Q

The assured results of source criticism, the two-source hypothesis, opened the way for an entirely new set of problems. If we accept this hypothesis as a solution to the problem of the literary interrelation of the Synoptics, the next question is: how did the material come down to Mark and Q? Or, in other words, what is the prehistory of the gospel material?

Two important factors are involved here. First, scholars had already recognized that the Synoptics were composed of smaller units (especially when compared with John) each of which could be viewed independently. For example, the story of the feeding of the five thousand is a relatively short paragraph in the Synoptics (Mk. 6:32–44 and par), while in John this incident is expanded into a long chapter (John 6) in which Jesus discusses the meaning of the event and its implications. Each separate event, saying, or narrative in the Synoptics could be considered a self-contained, independent item (or unit of tradition). The Fourth Gospel cannot be read in such a way; it is a much more cohesive and interconnected account which, from a literary point of view, flows quite smoothly. In contrast, the Synoptics appear to be choppy and less integrated. Second, the study of the Old Testament and folk literature had already suggested the importance of a period of oral transmission of material. These two factors could be combined to suggest that the pre-Markan situation was one in which small self-sufficient units of material could be circulated orally before being written down. Mark stands at the end of the period of oral transmission; he records the tradition he received. Historically, this means that if Mark was written about 66–70 A.D., the period between the death of Jesus (about 30) and the writing of Mark would be a time during which these short units were circulated by word of mouth.

FORM CRITICISM

With the advent of the form-critical analysis of the Synoptics and its emphasis on the oral stages of transmission, attention was focused on the *Sitz im Leben* of the early communities.[12] Some form critics

12. Form criticism is discussed in most introductions to the New Testament. For a

hoped to be able to work back through the material influenced by the developing church to the situation in the life of Jesus in which an incident or saying originally occurred. However, that goal was not reached,[13] and attention shifted to the situation of the early church. At present there are three *Sitze* which form critics will discuss: (1) the situation of the ancient church, (2) the situation in the life of Jesus, and (3) the situation of the evangelist.[14] The third *Sitz* is the most recently emphasized and is the focal point of redaction criticism. Form criticism is most at home working with larger narrative-based units. The pronouncement is a readily identifiable form and is easily handled by this approach. This is also the case with the much larger unit, the passion story. It is also true of the miracle story, legend, and parable. But form critics had less success with the general category of "sayings." Sayings do not have any narrative introductions and thus contain no easy clues (as form critics would define them) about their application by the people who used them. Most scholars followed Bultmann's lead in classifying them in five groups: (1) proverbs, (2) prophetic and apocalyptic sayings, (3) laws and community regulations, (4) "I" sayings, and (5) parables.[15]

The parable is an exception. Following the early hints of Jülicher[16] and Dodd,[17] J. Jeremias, a conservative form critic, was successful in applying form-critical methods to show how the parables had been used for different purposes at various stages in their transmission from the time of Jesus to the time of final recording by the evangelists.[18] Jeremias had such success in this analysis that his work is determinative for those form critics still interested in recovering the authentic sayings of Jesus.

---

basic (though conservative) view see Edgar V. McKnight, *What Is Form Criticism?* Guides to Biblical Scholarship (Philadelphia: Fortress Press, 1969), and his annotated bibliography, pp. 80–86.

13. For a survey of the problem and a summary of the results see Norman Perrin, *Rediscovering the Teaching of Jesus;* also, Hans Conzelmann, *Jesus* (Philadelphia: Fortress Press, 1974).

14. Willi Marxsen, *Mark, the Evangelist* (Nashville: Abingdon Press, 1969), p. 23.

15. Rudolf Bultmann, *The History of the Synoptic Tradition* (New York: Harper & Row, 1963), pp. 69–205.

16. A. Jülicher, *Die Gleichnisreden Jesu* (Tübingen, 1899).

17. C. H. Dodd, *The Parables of the Kingdom* (London: Nisbet, 1935).

18. Jeremias, *Parables.*

However, with the other four "sayings" categories, the problem is greater. It is much more difficult to apply the method used so successfully on the parables to these sayings. Most often they are too limited in scope and length to enable one to uncover a history of their use by the church. Also, their similarity in form and content to Jewish wisdom, prophetic, apocalyptic, and legal traditions, precludes their usefulness in the search for the truly distinctive features of the New Testament. As a result, they tend to be ignored by form critics. And because Q is composed primarily of sayings, the form-critical neglect of Q is natural.

Thus the form critics ignore Q, for the most part, because of its content and also because of their interest in the period prior to the time of writing. If Mark and Q are the two basic written sources (as the two-source hypothesis argues) we really need to go back behind them into the oral tradition. Dibelius did offer some comments about Q in a chapter entitled "Exhortation."[19] Contrasting Q to Mark, he recognized the existence of a need in the early commentary to collect the sayings of Jesus. By analogy to Paul, the sayings would most likely be used to instruct Christians, particularly those "of heathen origin."[20] The purpose of a collection of sayings such as Q, says Dibelius, is not to present a life of Jesus but "to give his words in order that they may be followed and in order that they may instruct."[21] A practical need for ethical guidance called forth this collection; there were problems which had to be solved, rules which had to be established. "It is perfectly certain that the sayings were not brought together at first for the sake of their Christological interest."[22] Dibelius's conclusion about the origins of Q is thus not significantly different from that of the source critic's.

REDACTION CRITICISM

When form criticism appeared to have reached an impasse in its search for the *Sitz im Leben* of Jesus, it was recognized that there had been a neglect of the other side of the tradition, the *Sitz im Leben*

19. Martin Dibelius, *From Tradition to Gospel*, trans. Bertram L. Woolf (New York: Charles Scribner's Sons, 1935), pp. 233–265.
20. Ibid., p. 239.
21. Ibid. p. 245.
22. Ibid. p. 246.

of the gospel writer (evangelist).[23] If the analysis of the individual units had been carried as far as possible, can anything be gained by an examination of the framework into which the tradition has been set? There had been little interest in this question up to this point because it was assumed that the evangelists were merely recording notes from the past. As Dibelius put it, the evangelists were "collectors"—arrangers of units of tradition.[24] Bultmann had argued that Mark was really not in control of his material, that he merely acted as the final editor who solidified tradition which had already taken shape.[25]

However, it quickly became clear that there was a great deal of leeway for an editor in such circumstances. In fact, the editor, or redactor, could mold the tradition in two ways: (1) by making changes in the unit itself and (2) by the order of his arrangement of the units. For the purposes of this discussion, I suggest that we label these two aspects of redaction criticism (1) emendation analysis and (2) composition analysis.

Emendation analysis is a direct result of the form critic's use of the synoptic parallels first developed by source critics. Since form criticism had established the possibility of the modification of material (against the source critics' assumption of fixed documents), the variations in wording which are evident through the use of a synopsis could be the result of the evangelist's editorial activity and not the result of a community modification at an earlier stage in the transmission of the tradition. It is this inter-synoptic analysis (emendation analysis) which appeared first in the development of redaction criticism.

Perhaps one of the clearest and earliest examples of this approach is the analysis by G. Bornkamm[26] of "Stilling the Storm." Bornkamm noted that Matthew has reversed the order of events. The actual performance of the miracle in Mark (4:39) and Luke (8:24) takes place before Jesus' questioning of the disciples. In Matthew the question is asked in the midst of the storm (8:25–6) *before* it is quelled.

23. Cf. Norman Perrin, *What Is Redaction Criticism?* (Philadelphia: Fortress Press, 1969).
24. Dibelius, *Tradition,* p. 59.
25. Bultmann, *History,* p. 332.
26. G. Bornkamm, G. Barth, H. J. Held, *Tradition and Interpretation in Matthew* (Philadelphia: Westminister Press, 1963), pp. 52–57.

STILLING THE STORM

Mt. 8:18	*Mk. 4:35–41*	*Lk. 8:22–25*
(18) Now when Jesus saw great crowds around him, he gave orders to go over to the other side. *Mt. 8:23–27* (23) And when he got into the boat, his disciples followed him. (24) And behold, there arose a great storm on the sea, so that the boat was being swamped by the waves; but he was asleep. (25) And they went and woke him, saying, "Save, Lord; we are perishing" (26) And he said to them, "Why are you afraid, O men of little faith?" Then he rose and rebuked the winds and the sea; and there was a great calm. (27) And the men marveled, saying, "What sort of man is this, that even winds and sea obey him?"	(35) On that day, when evening had come, he said to them, "Let us go across to the other side." (36) And leaving the crowd, they took him with them, just as he was, in the boat. And other boats were with him. (37) And a great storm of wind arose, and the waves beat into the boat, so that the boat was already filling. (38) But he was in the stern, asleep on the cushion; and they woke him and said to him, "Teacher, do you not care if we perish?" (39) And he awoke and rebuked the wind, and said to the sea, "Peace! Be still!" And the wind ceased, and there was a great calm. (40) He said to them, "Why are you afraid? Have you no faith?" (41) And they were filled with awe, and said to one another, "Who then is this, that even wind and sea obey him?"	(22) One day he got into a boat with his disciples, and he said to them, "Let us go across to the other side of the lake." So they set out, (23) and as they sailed he fell asleep. And a storm of wind came down on the lake, and they were filling with water, and were in danger. (24) And they went and woke him, saying, "Master, Master, we are perishing!" And he awoke and rebuked the wind and the raging waves; and they ceased, and there was a calm. (25) He said to them, "Where is your faith?" And they were afraid, and they marveled, saying to one another, "Who then is this, that he commands even wind and water, and they obey him?"

By this rearrangement, Bornkamm suggests, Matthew interprets the story in a parabolic sense: Jesus addresses men in the midst of their troubles before the final calm of the eschatological event. Matthew has also changed the title by which the disciples address Jesus (from Mark's "teacher" to "Lord"), with the result that the request becomes a prayer ("Save, Lord"). Jesus' response to the disciples is not only placed after the miracle, but is now a question about "men of little faith" rather than Mark's "Have you no faith?" A typical Matthean word is added at the beginning when Matthew explicitly says that the disciples "followed him" into the boat thereby emphasizing the significance of this unit for a definition of discipleship. Each of these changes contributes toward making the Markan miracle story a new entity in Matthew. By his emending of the details in Mark, a new meaning is implied.

Emendation analysis can only function, however, when there is a clear distinction between tradition and redaction, when we have a precise knowledge of the sources. In this case Matthew's basic dependence is upon Mark. Hans Conzelmann's famous study of Luke applies the same emendation analysis technique throughout the Gospel of Luke to argue that Luke's theology can be characterized by, among other things, a new and adjusted eschatology, an eschatology which views the parousia as being delayed.[27] The power of Conzelmann's work lies in the accumulation of evidence from many examples of both additions and especially deletions in Luke's use of Mark.

Because Mark is a primary source, we do not have any documentary evidence of *his* sources, making the distinction between tradition and redaction in Mark a much more complex one. W. Marxsen suggested that the uniqueness of Mark could be highlighted by carefully watching the way Matthew and Luke redact Mark.[28] Thus, by using a triangulation technique one might be able to come somewhat closer to the redaction of Mark. Marxsen's analysis was eagerly received but has not produced the certainty which many hoped for. Emendation analysis is primarily a method used in the study of Matthew and Luke. Some other approach is necessary for Mark.

It was not long before the similarity of the problem of redactional analysis of Mark and Acts was noticed. Neither book has any earlier sources with which it can be compared. Instead, it is necessary to approach these works by an analysis of their structure or composition. E. Haenchen suggested the name "composition criticism" as a result of his work on both Acts and Mark.[29] Since it is assumed that

---

27. Hans Conzelmann, *The Theology of St. Luke* (New York: Harper & Row, 1961). Eschatology is treated in part two, pp. 95–136.
28. Willi Marxsen, *Mark*, pp. 25–29.
29. Ernst Haenchen, *Die Apostelgeschichte* (Kritisch-Exegetischer Kommentar über das Neue Testament. Dritte Abteilung, 14. Auflage) (Göttingen: Vandenhoeck und Ruprecht, 1965). Ernst Haenchen, *Der Weg Jesu* (Berlin: Töpelmann, 1966). The phrase "composition criticism" was suggested on p. 24.

the tradition was available in isolated units or in small collections of units, the contribution of the editor or final author is illustrated by his arrangement (composing) of the tradition.

One of the most impressive examples of this approach is the recognition of a threefold pattern in Mk. 8:27–10:45: three predictions of the passion, followed by a misunderstanding of the implications of the prediction, and followed each time by a collection of teachings of Jesus which is meant to correct the misunderstanding. This pattern occurs just prior to the passion story itself.[30]

1. Prediction of the Son of Man's Suffering—8:31; 9:31; 10:33
2. Misunderstanding—8:32–33; 9:33–37; 10:35–40
3. Teaching—8:34–9:29; 9:38–10:30; 10:41–45

The refocusing of attention upon the later stages of the history of the tradition (the redaction of the evangelist) opens up the possibility of a return to the study of Q. But the methodological issue is still unsolved. We cannot compare Q with an earlier source—so emendation study is ruled out. Nor is composition analysis possible until we have a clear knowledge of the order of Q, and as indicated previously, we cannot be sure of this. V. Taylor argued that the order of Q in Luke was probably very close to the original. But this hypothesis is based upon a previous hypothesis about Matthew's editorial techniques which is not universally accepted. It seems best for the present to proceed on the assumption that the original arrangement is unknown. But, before a solution to this problem of the theology of Q can be suggested it is necessary to review briefly the redaction-critical work which placed the Q material in the spotlight once again.

H. E. TÖDT

As a result of his study of the Son of Man title in the synoptic tradition, H. E. Tödt was led by the evidence to a consideration of Q as a theological entity.[31]

---

30. Norman Perrin, *Redaction Criticism,* pp. 40–63.
31. H. E. Tödt, *The Son of Man in the Synoptic Tradition* (Philadelphia: Westminster Press, 1965).

His study of the Son of Man is a history of the traditions in which the phrase appears. Tödt accepts the current scholarly convention, established by Bultmann, of distinguishing between three groups of Son of Man sayings.[32] The "present" sayings imply that Jesus is *now* the Son of Man in his activity on earth in his ministry. The "coming" sayings refer to the Son of Man as a figure of the future, at the time of the judgment, who may be the same person as Jesus. The "suffering" sayings refer to the suffering and death of the Son of Man. Tödt emphasized the Markan character of the "suffering" Son of Man material and thus was forced to consider the possibility of a Son of Man theology which was expressed in "present" and "future" Son of Man sayings only. He was already convinced of the earliness and authenticity of the "future" sayings by the work of Bultmann. Q contains both "future" and "present" sayings (but no "suffering" sayings) and Tödt concluded that Q represented a tradition in the early church in which an original "Christological cognition" had taken place—i.e., where Jesus was recognized both as the coming Son of Man and where "present-activity sayings were first formulated."[33] Jesus *will be* the Son of Man and, in fact, he *now is* the Son of Man. From a post-Easter perspective, Jesus' true character as Son of Man during his earthly career can be affirmed.

If Q does represent such a theological and christological point of view, a conclusion Dibelius would deny, then the Q community might represent a very influential and distinct stage in the development of the synoptic tradition. If this is possible, the widely accepted distinction between *kerygma* and *didache* must be reexamined. If Dodd's understanding of the *kerygma* is correct, the Q material is *didache* and thus of secondary importance in understanding early Christianity. The questions which Tödt raised were: What kind of community would be interested in a collection of sayings of Jesus which does not contain any reference to the passion? What kind of Christology is implied in this "limited" approach?

Tödt's solution was the suggestion that an early community could have conceived of its task as that of continuing to speak the words of Jesus rather than preaching about him. Their message is not Dodd's

32. Ibid., p. 17.
33. Ibid., pp. 226–269 (see esp. p. 231).

kerygma but a quite different one, the repetition of Jesus' words, which was subsequently absorbed into the Pauline suffering and death *kerygma*. The Q community's recognition of Jesus as the Son of Man (their interpretation of the Easter event) means that they are to continue his work until his return—obviously assumed to be in the near future. Since Q does not have a "suffering" Son of Man Christology, their concern is not his death but his continued presence among those who acknowledge him and await his return.[34]

In this manner, Tödt opened an entirely new set of possibilities for the study of Q and the Q community. There was already a growing awareness of the significant diversity among the early communities of Christianity which was related to the recognition of the influence of Luke-Acts in presenting a one-sided view of the early church. When Tödt suggested a non-Pauline style of Christology which could be established on the basis of biblical material, the general reaction was favorable. Yet Tödt's concern with the Son of Man limited his interest in Q and he never developed his suggestions about the full scope of the theology of Q. However, his work stands as a major turning point and was an impetus for the growing number of studies of Q. He demonstrated quite effectively how important the redaction-critical approach could be in the search for the early church.

In the following chapters we shall affirm the basic conclusions of Tödt but at the same time look further and more thoroughly into the character of the Q community. In that process many of the more recent studies of Q will be used to help establish the main contours of the theology of this early community.

A corollary of form criticism is that the existence of oral tradition is dependent upon a group of people and not merely an individual. Although an individual may be the "creator" or originator of a specific item, its preservation will depend upon its acceptance and use by others. Throughout this study, the phrase "community of Q" is used to designate the people responsible for the preservation of the Q material—prior to the time when Matthew and Luke incorporated it into their Gospels. It is assumed that oral literature emerges from a specific context.

---

34. Ibid., esp. pp. 246–253.

Although redaction criticism emphasizes the final editor and his work in molding the tradition, the nonexistence of a text of Q which is independent of Matthew and Luke makes it impossible to arrive at precise distinctions. Thus the search is for a community which preserved Q and not the individual responsible for its final form (because the "final form" does not exist as such).

As will be explained later, this community would be a group of like-minded individuals who use the Q material in their activities. Because it is important to them, their attitudes and ideas can be reconstructed by working back from their writings. There is not enough information available to enable one to locate them in a specific time or place. Q is *not*, then, a designation for the people of the Dead Sea Scrolls at Qumran. Both are apocalyptic groups, but their literary remains are quite different and reflect very different religious beliefs.

By the time we have looked more carefully at the Q material, we will be in a good position to suggest some specific characteristics of the Q community.

II

CHOOSING A METHOD

A close examination of New Testament scholarship of the past two decades will reveal the importance of a carefully thought-out and conscious understanding of method. It has become increasingly clear that the results of an investigation depend very largely on the questions which are asked. As a result, scholars will usually preface their work with a precise statement of their understanding of the problem and their means for solving it. We have already seen that the acceptance of the *"kerygma-didache"* distinction had the effect of focusing attention on Mark and away from Q. When emphasis later shifted toward form criticism, the new assumption of an oral period of literary transmission resulted in a new and varied assessment of the material which had been "thoroughly" analyzed previously. A clear statement of how one intends to *approach* (and possibly solve) a question about literary material will assist the reader in following the argument. This is especially true in any attempt to understand a tradition such as Q which is itself the product of an hypothesis. If the following analysis of Q is to be given serious consideration, it is imperative that the lines of approach be fully explained and consciously tested.

This study of the theology of Q is the outgrowth of a conscious application of the redaction-critical method. However, as previously stated, the two primary styles of redaction analysis (emendation and composition) are not directly applicable. Emendation analysis assumes that we have some controls which allow us to pinpoint precisely the modifications of an earlier source or tradition. With Q, these sources do not exist. Composition analysis, which has been used so widely and creatively in the study of Mark and Acts, is also ruled out by the fact that the arrangement of Q cannot be firmly ascertained. How then can we proceed?

As we have seen, Tödt opened up the possibility of viewing Q as a viable, theological, self contained entity with his study of the title "Son of Man."[1] If other titles are prominent in Q, we might be able to discover other traditions developing in Q, but to date, that approach has not been successful. Because Q is primarily a sayings-source, it will have to be the sayings themselves which supply the primary information.

James M. Robinson proposed a category, *Logoi Sophōn* (Sayings of the Wise), based in part on the similarity between the newly discovered Gospel of Thomas and Q.[2] Thomas is a collection of the sayings of Jesus and claims to be a gospel but does not contain any account of the passion nor does it contain any narrative section. The order of the sayings is not integrated into any plot as is typical of the canonical Gospels. Robinson asks whether there is any precedent for such a collection of isolated sayings and what the purpose of such a collection might be.

His conclusion was that such a *Gattung* or form of literature already existed in Jewish traditions as the collection of the sayings of a wise man in such books as Proverbs and Pirke Aboth and also in apocalyptic literature in Enoch. Q might then be viewed as a part of a larger "trajectory" which has its beginnings in these Jewish writings, and is later developed in Gnostic circles as the Gospel of Thomas. In the last, Jesus is considered to be a sage who is important because his insight is superior to that of other men. The origins of this approach might be ascribed to a variety of reasons which would have to be discovered by a close analysis of the peculiar character of the Q sayings themselves and related to earlier and later collections.

We have no similar independent elaboration of this *Gattung* in the canonical material. Q itself has been absorbed into the gospel

1. H. E. Tödt, *The Son of Man in the Synoptic Tradition* (Philadelphia: Westminster Press, 1965).
2. James M. Robinson, "Logoi Sophon: On the Gattung of Q," in J. M. Robinson and H. Koester, *Trajectories through Early Christianity* (Philadelphia: Fortress Press, 1971), pp. 71–113.

genre and interwoven with the extensive narrative materials of Mark by both Matthew and Luke. Nonetheless, it does reappear in a modified form in the "heretical" collection of the sayings of the resurrected Lord in Thomas and Pistis Sophia. Robinson did not go on to examine the content of Q in this article but elsewhere he suggested that the material in Q *could* be viewed from the later Gnosticizing tendency.[3] This means that a collection which Matthew and Luke consider legitimate is transformed by the Gnostic point of view into a statement of the faith which the later church would not accept. He thus proposes that Q is best understood as a book of the acts of Wisdom.

Robinson's work does more to whet than to satisfy our appetite. His recognition of a possible *Gattung* and a sayings trajectory helps to clear the way for more detailed analysis. It is an important step in showing the historical context for such a collection of sayings; it establishes a foundation for the growing interest in Q as a different approach to Jesus, different from the gospel *Gattung*.

The imperialism of the *kerygma* as defined by Dodd has now been effectively challenged. Although they are working with quite different methods, Tödt and Robinson have cleared the way for a study of the Q material as the remnants of a community with a self-consistent theological stance. Both within the material itself (Tödt) and in the context of first-century literary traditions (Robinson) Q is seen as a positive theological factor and not merely as a secondary collection of simple *didache*.

The next step would appear to be the search for basic themes or consistent topics in the materials. If Q is approached from this angle, the most obvious theme is its eschatological attitude. The recognition of this theme is quite a reversal from the earlier judgments about Q's basic moral and catechetical traditions. One would expect to find a collection of sayings, which was supposedly to offer advice about how to live in the world as a converted Christian, surrounded by a highly developed expectation of the imminent end of this age. And yet the eschatology here is more than a theme—it is a basic mood or attitude which permeates every part of the material. This character-

3. J. M. Robinson, "Jesus as Sophos and Sophia; Wisdom Tradition and the Gospels" (unpublished paper delivered at Notre Dame University, 1972).

istic of the Q material could have been expected, of course, in the light of Tödt's stress upon the central significance of the Son of Man title. Once the initial openness to Q was established, the individuality of the material could be seriously considered.

Howard Kee discusses the content of Q in chapter 3 of his book *Jesus in History*.[4] His approach is one of searching for themes or subjects which occur with consistency in the sayings. He finds one narrative and merely three parenetic (exhortatory) sayings, while all the rest (thirty-seven) are eschatological. His analysis of the individual sayings stresses the pervasiveness of eschatology—it seems to have permeated every kind of material. The positive achievement of this study is its help in focusing attention on the eschatology of Q, but there is little progress toward a reconstruction of the theology or the *Sitz* of the community.

Dieter Lührmann's *Die Redaktion der Logienquelle* is the first lengthy study of Q following the work of Tödt.[5] His contribution is a systematic application of redaction-critical methods to the Q material. Since emendation analysis is not possible, Lührmann makes a distinction between the collecting and editing activity of the author(s). This distinction affords him the opportunity of uncovering layers of material. Because Q is a collection of sayings (each collection having existed independently at first), one must look for the earlier collections which have not been fragmented by Matthew and Luke. Thus, where Matthew and Luke exhibit a similar *order* of sayings, we can assume that this order is based on the Q collection. A second source of insight into the Q theology can be found where we have a partially parallel passage in Mark. If Matthew and Luke agree in placing the same Q material into the same place in the Markan outline, it is likely that Q contained the same basic story. In these cases, then, Lührmann highlights the differences between Mark and Q and claims added insight into the distinctiveness of Q.

Lührmann is not consistent in this approach, however. As he himself indicates, his is primarily an attempt to show that there can be some significant progress made toward an understanding of Q.

4. Howard C. Kee, *Jesus in History* (New York: Harcourt, Brace & World, 1970), pp. 62–103.
5. Dieter Lührmann, *Die Redaktion der Logienquelle,* WMANT 33 (Neukirchen-Vluyn: Neukirchener Verlag, 1969).

His results are tentative and sketchy because they are not based upon a study of the full document; he is still looking for an opening or method which will do full justice to the distinctive character of the material itself and to the complexity of the problem. Although we will return later to some of Lührmann's analyses, some of his general conclusions need to be noted now.

The most unexpected conclusion is his claim that the evidence points toward a situation for the Q community in which the delay of the parousia has become a major consideration. To suggest this for a community prior to 66–70 A.D. is unusual indeed.

The basis for this conclusion is his distinction between the watchfulness of Mark over against the advice in Q to *use* the time which remains until the Lord returns. This emphasis, in combination with the emphasis on judgment at the end, leads Lührmann to the conclusion that the Q community is indeed an eschatological one, but one which has recognized the time before the end as having a new significance—because the end is "delayed." It seems unlikely, however, that such a conclusion is possible even if the original assumptions are granted. In any imminent eschatology, there must be some time between the now and the end. It could be a time of action in preparing for the end rather than a consciousness of a delay. In addition, the prior assumptions about a vast difference between watchfulness and the use of the "last days" does not seem appropriate particularly in a Jewish environment.

The Q community, says Lührmann, which lies behind this material is one in which Jesus' words are of prime importance. The emphasis of these words is on discipleship which is especially evident in what Lührmann considers the opening speech, the beatitudes. Judgment sayings are frequent and illustrate Q's opposition to "this generation," which Lührmann interprets as the people of Israel. Lührmann also sees some indications of a Hellenistic environment. But the judgment theme is crucial in Lührmann's reconstruction and helps to reassure the community of its safety at the appearance of the Kingdom. He mentions that wisdom forms are present and yet that Jesus is not identified or personified as wisdom. Moreover, he suggests that apocalyptic and wisdom should be recognized as "interacting." Lührmann's work is suggestive at many points but is too sketchy to have established much more than an indication of where some fruitful contributions might be made.

In 1972 the second major work on Q appeared—*Studien zur Theologie der Logienquelle* by Paul Hoffmann.[6] Hoffmann reacts to the work of both Tödt and Lührmann and thus has the opportunity of developing the discussion in a significant way. He consciously limits himself to selected topics which bear directly on the problem of developing a complete, overall theology of the community but he does not attempt to formulate such an overview. This lack is, in my opinion, the most disappointing aspect of the book.

There are three studies in the book—on eschatology, on the Son of Man, and on the messengers of Jesus. Hoffmann's method is to examine all those sections of Q which might shed some light on the major issue. As a result, any one passage might be considered in a number of places in the text.

In Part One, Hoffmann is engaged in conversation primarily with D. Lührmann who sees the Q community influenced by the delay of the parousia. Hoffmann disagrees. He finds a basic agreement between the expectation of the Q community and the immediate expectation expressed by John the Baptist. Jesus, however, is pictured as the coming judge as well as the herald of the end. For Q, John marks the beginning of the end, an end which is yet to come (though in the near future) when the Son of Man returns. This conclusion is supported by a careful examination of selected pericopes from Q which Hoffmann deems relevant to the theme. Each major pericope is given lengthy attention and secondary pericopes are mentioned. The reconstruction of the text of Q is always viewed in the light of Matthean or Lukan redaction.

Part Two is primarily concerned with A. G. Polag's contention that Q's Christology is both late and functional[7] and with D. Lührmann's de-emphasis on the Son of Man. Hoffmann, agreeing with Tödt, emphasizes the future dimension of the title. Easter has intensified the community's expectation about the coming prophetic-

---

6. Paul Hoffmann, *Studien zur Theologie der Logienquelle,* Neutestamentliche Abhandlungen, n. f. 8 (Münster: Aschendorff, 1972).
7. A. Polag, "Der Umfang der Logienquelle" (unpublished dissertation, Treves, 1966).

charismatic teacher who was to appear as Son of Man. Whether or not one can agree that the future element is "all important," Hoffmann has presented a strong case for the significance of the future expectation as a way of giving meaning to the historical Jesus and his sayings.

Part Three is the most interesting section of the book. It is primarily an analysis of the text of the mission speech (Lk. 10:2–16, 21–22 and par.). Hoffmann finds here an imminent eschatology in the mission which will awaken people to the nearness of the expected return of the Son of Man (against Lührmann). A major Q emphasis is the distinction between rejection and persecution, based on the experiences of John and Jesus and anticipating problems which the messengers can expect.

The Q community, says Hoffmann, considers itself related to the eschatological prophet tradition—combining elements of the Deuteronomic tradition[8] and wisdom teaching. But these tendencies are rooted in Jesus' own self-understanding and in his work. Since the Son of Man material is the ground and not the content of the message of Q, the message which is preached is the urgent need to act upon the basis of Jesus' words.

Hoffmann breaks new ground in suggesting that a possible historical context of the Q community might be their opposition to the Zealots. The basis of this suggestion is the speaking of "Peace" and the reference to collecting the "Sons of Peace" (Lk. 10:5–6). The neglect of such an emphasis in subsequent traditions is, of course, due to its lack of relevancy outside Palestine.

Despite all the insight evident in Hoffmann's work, one must question whether it is possible to move toward a theology of a disconnected and scattered collection such as Q without a more comprehensive view of the material and its themes. Hoffmann has succeeded in making us aware of some basic themes in the material, but I am not satisfied that this piecemeal approach can really help unless we have an integrated understanding of the entire collection. Hoffmann at times seems to be aware of this. If one approaches his book

8. O. H. Steck, *Israel und das gewaltsame Geschick der Propheten*, WMANT 23 (Neukirchen-Vluyn: Neukirchener Verlag, 1967).

as a series of sketches, which might need serious correction later when more material is included as primary consideration, it will be a very useful addition to the redactional task.

THE TASK

The method used in this study is one which combines a variety of the suggestions already mentioned. It begins with a basic form-critical analysis but, following the kind of approach suggested by Käsemann,[9] it concentrates on forms which are smaller and more grammatically defined than the traditional forms of form criticism (viz. apophthegms, tales, miracle stories, sayings, etc.). When these smaller forms have been identified, the next step is to note carefully the themes and emphases contained in the forms. As we will see, it is not possible to distinguish clearly between form and content and very often an emphasis may be expressed in a variety of forms. However, this interplay of form and content will be used to help isolate the basic interests of the community responsible for collecting the Q material. Of particular interest will be the contrast between this material and the other non-Q synoptic material as well as the traditions of the Jewish community at large. This aspect of the method is in part dependent upon the criterion of "distinctiveness" or "dissimilarity" which has been developed in the form-critical search for authentic sayings of Jesus.[10] Our concern is to uncover the theology of the Q community, however, and not to solve the problem of whether these sayings originate with Jesus or the community.

Since Q is composed almost entirely of sayings, these shorter forms are various types of sayings. We will be attempting to differentiate between statements in terms of both form and content (or structure and theme). If this can be done, we ought to have a clear picture of the emphases of the community: when they repeat Jesus'

9. Ernst Käsemann, "Sentence of Holy Law in the New Testament," in *New Testament Questions of Today* (Philadelphia: Fortress Press, 1969), pp. 66–81. The method used in this study resulted from Käsemann's definition of a *Satz heiligen Rechts*. See R. A. Edwards, *The Sign of Jonah in the Theology of the Evangelists and Q*, Studies in Biblical Theology, #18 Second Series (London: SCM Press, 1971), pp. 52–53.
10. Clearly stated in Norman Perrin, *Rediscovering the Teaching of Jesus* (New York: Harper & Row, 1967), pp. 39–43.

sayings, what meaning or thrust do the sayings have which would help to clarify the user's intention in repeating them?

Some examples of the shorter forms in Luke are:

1. Beatitude:

> 13:35b—"And I tell you, you will not see me until you say, 'Blessed be he who comes in the name of the Lord!' "

2. Woe:

> 17:1—And he said to his disciples, "Temptations to sin are sure to come; but woe to him by whom they come!"

3. Parable:

> 11:24–26—"When the unclean spirit has gone out of a man, he passes through waterless places seeking rest; and finding none he says, 'I will return to my house from which I came.' And when he comes he finds it swept and put in order. Then he goes and brings seven other spirits more evil than himself, and they enter and dwell there; and the last state of that man becomes worse than the first."

4. Eschatological pronouncement saying:

> 12:8–9—"And I tell you, every one who acknowledges me before men, the Son of man also will acknowledge before the angels of God; but he who denies me before men will be denied before the angels of God."

5. Eschatological correlative:

> 11:30—"For as Jonah became a sign to the men of Nineveh, so will the Son of man be to this generation."

6. Conditional relative:

> 12:10—"And every one who speaks a word against the Son of man will be forgiven; but he who blasphemes against the Holy Spirit will not be forgiven."

7. Proverb:

> 12:2—"Nothing is covered up that will not be revealed, or hidden that will not be known."

8. Prophetic pronouncement:

> 11:39—And the Lord said to him, "Now you Pharisees cleanse the outside of the cup and of the dish, but inside you are full of extortion and wickedness."

With this data as a foundation, we can then ask how these structures and themes can be put together to reconstruct the theology of the community which preserves them.

III

ESCHATOLOGY

Eschatology has been one of the major issues in NT studies for over seventy years. It is a term which has been used in many different ways and to support many varied points of view. The tendency in biblical studies has been to modify it with such terms as "realized," "consistent," "imminent," etc. Because our concern here is with Q, it will be necessary to make only a brief survey of the history of the term before we turn to the Q material. Since this topic is most often discussed in reference to the Kingdom of God sayings, we will use that as a point of focus.

Consistent Eschatology

Johannes Weiss initiated the modern discussion of eschatology with a series of books in 1892–1900.[1] In reacting to the analysis of the Kingdom of God by Ritschl, he argues that Jesus conceived of the Kingdom as a breaking out of an overpowering divine storm which erupts into history to destroy and to renew, and which a man can neither further nor influence.[2] Jesus does not present a new teaching

---

1. Johannes Weiss, *Die Predigt Jesu vom Reiche Gottes* (Göttingen: Vandenhoeck & Ruprecht, 1892); *Die Idee des Reiches Gottes in der Theologie* (Giessen: J. Ricker'sche, 1900); *Die Predigt Jesu vom Reiche Gottes,* 2d ed. (Göttingen: Vandenhoeck & Ruprecht, 1900), English translation: *Jesus' Proclamation of the Kingdom of God,* Lives of Jesus Series (Philadelphia: Fortress Press, 1971).
2. Norman Perrin, *The Kingdom of God in the Teaching of Jesus* (Philadelphia: Westminster Press, 1963), p. 18. This book is a good survey of the rise of interest in the eschatological dimension of Jesus' teaching.

about the Kingdom of God but the certainty that Satan has fallen and the world is in God's hand.[3] Thus Jesus must be understood in the context of prophetic and apocalyptic Judaism.

According to Weiss, Jesus expected the Kingdom of God in the immediate future. It is a Kingdom which God brings and which is breaking into the present (Jesus' present) and which is to be understood as a contrast to the ways of men. The new age is not a continuation of the present but the turn of the ages. Thus Jesus' ethical teaching was not an attempt to establish the right environment for the coming of the Kingdom, but an explication of the conditions of entry into the Kingdom when it does come. "The ethical teaching is designed to explicate what is involved in the repentance which the imminence of the Kingdom demands."[4] This analysis is related to Jesus' choice of the title "Son of Man" which is a vague term used in his time to imply a future, unspecific figure; it demonstrates his own uncertainty about his role.

Richard Hiers writes the following interesting comment about the implications of Weiss's work:

> Weiss was quite aware that recognizing the echatological character of Jesus' conception of the kingdom of God would make it no longer possible to maintain that the words and outlook of the historical Jesus and the late-nineteenth-century theological interpretation of Jesus and his message were one and the same. He insists, therefore, that ". . . we cannot any longer use Jesus' words in the exact sense that was originally intended."[5]

Albert Schweitzer subsequently developed the views of Weiss.[6] Schweitzer emphasized the ethical implication of this "consistent eschatology" and first used the phrase "interim ethics." Depending primarily on Matthew 10 in contrast to the passion narrative, he pictures Jesus as a tragic figure who hoped to force the coming of the Kingdom—and failed. Although many of the details of Schweitzer's reconstruction are rejected today, his influence is considerable

---

3. Ibid., p. 19.
4. Ibid., p. 22.
5. Richard H. Hiers, *The Kingdom of God in the Synoptic Tradition,* University of Florida Humanities Monograph 33 (Gainesville: University of Florida Press, 1970), p. 9.
6. Albert Schweitzer, *The Quest of the Historical Jesus* (New York: Macmillan, 1959), pp. 238 ff.

because of his thorough use of the conclusions of Weiss. It is Schweitzer who is considered the primary representative of "consistent eschatology."

Realized Eschatology

In reaction to the emphasis on imminent eschatology, C. H. Dodd has argued that Jesus taught that the reality of the Kingdom of God was realized in his own ministry—thus the phrase "realized eschatology." Based on his analysis of the parables, Dodd argues that the crucial phase must be translated "the Kingdom of God *has come.*"[7] Any saying which has a future referent points to something beyond time and space, not to a future in this world; the Kingdom has come already in the ministry of Jesus. The crisis, which is so evident in the parables, is to be understood as the crisis of the present appearance of Jesus. Later layers of tradition have interpreted the crisis as the second coming—this was not the intention of Jesus.

There is a comparable change in the understanding of ethics. Rejecting interim ethics, Dodd sees Jesus' moral teaching as "a moral ideal for men who have accepted the Kingdom of God, and live their lives in the presence of his judgment and grace, now decisively revealed."[8]

Hiers refers to Dodd's method as one of reading into the material one's own interpretation by calling the language of Jesus (the eschatological imagery) a symbolic vehicle which was necessary for his own time.[9] Nonetheless, it is necessary to attempt to understand the material by whatever means we have available simply because we are no longer able to participate in the first-century environment. Although Dodd's realized eschatology is no longer widely accepted, it does demand our consideration.

Both Present and Future

A mediating point of view argues that both "future" and "realized" elements exist in the eschatology of Jesus and thus neither

---

7. C. H. Dodd, *The Parables of the Kingdom* (London: Nisbet, 1935.).
8. Ibid., p. 109.
9. Heirs, *Kingdom,* p. 13.

should be considered as the only possibility. J. Jeremias in his famous book on the parables argues that, since Jesus not only announces that the hour of fulfillment is here but, in addition, obviously expected a future in which the completion of God's action would be accomplished, it would be best to describe the eschatology of Jesus as "eschatology that is in the process of realization."[10] Thus both Jesus and the early church are correct—they anticipate a decisive event in the future and also realize the overwhelming significance of Jesus' ministry.

This compromise view is shared by W. Kümmel[11] and O. Cullmann,[12] among many others.[13]

Son of Man

The unusual phrase "Son of Man" found in the Gospels (and only once elsewhere in the New Testament—Acts 7) has been a prominent one in the discussion about eschatology. A complete survey of this complex problem can be found in a number of places.[14]

For our purposes, it is necessary to recognize that there are three kinds of Son of Man sayings which scholars have classified: (1) suffering sayings—in which death and dying is the primary activity of the Son of Man; (2) future sayings—in which the future appearance and activity of the Son of Man is stated; (3) present-activity sayings—in which the present pre-crucifixion action of the Son of Man on earth is emphasized.

The suffering sayings are found in Mark or in passages where Matthew and Luke are dependent on Mark and can therefore be assigned to the Markan layer of tradition; whether they are original with Mark or, as seems more likely, come from a tradition known to Mark, they are not found elsewhere. Q and Mark contain both present-activity sayings and future sayings.

Because the Son of Man is quite clearly an eschatological figure—a

---

10. Joachim Jeremias, *The Parables of Jesus,* rev. ed. (New York: Charles Scribner's Sons, 1963), p. 159.
11. W. G. Kümmel, *Promise and Fulfillment,* Studies in Biblical Theology 23 (London: SCM Press, 1961).
12. O. Cullmann, *Christ and Time* (Philadelphia: Westminster Press, 1950).
13. See Perrin, *Kingdom,* pp. 79–89.
14. Perrin, *Kingdom,* pp. 90–111. Tödt, *The Son of Man in the Synoptic Tradition* (Philadelphia: Westminster Press, 1965).

future judge who is expected in the last times—the discussion about eschatology has often hinged on one's interpretation of the Son of Man sayings. The most prominent interpretation is that of H. E. Tödt who argues that Jesus speaks about the future Son of Man as someone distinct from himself.[15] If this is correct, it is the Q community which has repeated these original sayings *and* added the present-activity sayings to clarify their assumptions that Jesus himself is the Son of Man. Others have argued that the Son of Man sayings all originate with the early church, that Jesus did not use the phrase at all.[16]

Assessments of the validity and meaning of the title are legion. Below, it will be suggested that the Q community probably created the present-activity sayings and may also have put into the mouth of Jesus the future Son of Man sayings. Nevertheless, authentic to Jesus or not, Son of Man is a prominent element in the eschatology of Q.

Existential Eschatology

Eschatology is an ambiguous word these days because of the work of Rudolf Bultmann.[17] He takes up the problem of eschatology and ethics, which had been raised since the time of Weiss, and develops an approach which takes full consideration of the first-century context for Jesus' thought and, at the same time, can interpret the apparently out-of-date material in a contemporary context. This amazing feat is accomplished by using the existentialist concept of "self-understanding." Jesus expressed his self-understanding in words and images which were current in his own time. The interpreter must find the "deeper meaning" in the first-century material and then express that meaning in words and images of *his* time. Existential philosophy supplies the means for making this transition.

Thus, for Bultmann, Jesus' eschatology is a statement of the crisis which each individual must face before an indefinite future. When Jesus announces that the Kingdom of God is at hand he is calling

---

15. Tödt, *Son of Man.*
16. Norman Perrin, *Rediscovering the Teaching of Jesus* (New York: Harper & Row, 1967), pp. 164–199.
17. Besides the summary in Perrin, *Kingdom,* pp. 112–129 see R. Bultmann, *Jesus and the Word* (New York: Charles Scribner's Sons, 1958) and *Jesus Christ and Mythology* (New York: Charles Scribner's Sons, 1958).

each person to recognize his need to rely on God and not on any earthly power or device. Authentic existence is the giving up of the self to the promise of a future controlled by God.

Bultmann's influence has been enormous and any discussion of eschatology since Bultmann must clarify its relation to him. Obviously not everyone is willing to accept Bultmann's proposal. But his influence has been so great that he must be considered.

ESCHATOLOGY IN Q

How does one show that there is an eschatological attitude or interest in any material? As noted above, Howard Kee finds the eschatological orientation of Q to be its decisive, distinguishing mark.[18] Citing Luke, he organizes that material as follows:

NARRATIVE MATERIAL
1.   Healing the Centurion's Slave (7:2, 6b–10)
PARENETIC MATERIAL
1.   Serving Two Masters (16:13)
2.   On Light or Darkness Within (11:34–36)
3.   On Faith and Forgiveness (17:3b–4, 6)
ESCHATOLOGICAL MATERIAL
Eschatological Warning
1.   Preaching Judgment (3:7–9)
2.   Baptism with Spirit and Fire (3:16–17)
3.   Judging and Eschatological Judgment (6:37–42)
4.   Woes on the Cities Where Jesus Performed Mighty Works (10:13–15)
5.   Judgment on the Scribes and Pharisees (11:39–52)
6.   Fire, Baptism, Sword, and Division (12:49–53)
7.   Inability to Interpret the Signs of This Time (12:54–56)
8.   Repent in View of the Impending Crisis (12:57–58)
9.   Prepare for the Crisis (13:24–29)
10. Lament over Jerusalem's Impending Doom (13:34–35)
11. Judgment on the Careless and Preoccupied (17:24, 26–27, 33–37)
Eschatological Conflict
1.   Contest with the Devil (4:2–12)
2.   Defeating the Prince of Demons (11:14–22)
3.   Dispelling the Unclean Spirits (11:23–26)

18. Howard Kee, *Jesus in History* (New York: Harcourt, Brace & World, 1970), pp. 71–73.

Eschatological Promise
1. The Beatitudes (6:20b–23)
2. Love of Enemies (6:27–36)
3. Eschatological Prayer (11:2–4)
4. What God Will Give (11:9–13)
5. Seek the Kingdom (12:22–31)
6. Treasures in Heaven (12:33–34)
7. A Role in the Kingdom (22:28–30)

Eschatological Knowledge
1. Gratitude for What God Has Revealed (10:21–24)

Eschatological Discipleship
1. Fitness for the Kingdom (9:57–60)
2. The Kingdom Has Drawn Near (10:2–12)
3. Fearless Confession (12:2–12)
4. Bearing the Cross (14:26–27)

Eschatological Parables
1. Three Parables of Watchfulness (12:39–40, 42–46)
2. Kingdom Compared with Leaven (13:20–21)
3. The Great Supper (14:16–23)
4. The Joyous Shepherd (15:4–7)
5. Investing the Pounds (19:11–27)
6. The Threatened House (6:47–49)

Jesus as Eschatological Messenger and Salvation-Bringer
1. Jesus' Ministry Fulfills Scripture (7:18–23)
2. John Is the Forerunner; Jesus Brings the Kingdom (7:24–35)
3. Law and Prophets Give Way to the Kingdom (16:16–17)
4. To Receive Jesus Is to Receive God (10:16)
5. Jesus = The Sign of Jonah: Prophet and Wise Man (11:29b–32)
6. Sitting at Jesus' Table in the Kingdom (14:15; 22:28–30)
7. Lament over Jerusalem Ends in Promise of Messiah's Coming (13:34–35; 19:41–44)

By dividing the material into "themes," Kee claims that only four of forty-three sections of Q are not directly eschatological—and he argues that these twenty-nine pericopes are "eschatological in content and intent."[19]

D. Lührmann also acknowledges (assumes) the thoroughly eschatological character of Q.[20] However, he sees evidence of a recognition of a delay in the appearance of the parousia.

---

19. Ibid., p. 91.
20. Dieter Lührmann, *Die Redaktion der Logienquelle*, WMANT 33 (Neukirchen-Vluyn: Neukirchener Verlag, 1969), pp. 69–83.

P. Hoffmann, on the other hand, argues that the eschatology of Q is an imminent one.[21] In response to Lührmann, he sees no evidence of a delay of the parousia; John is considered the one who is the beginning of the end, The final event is the future appearance of the Judge, the Son of Man, who is Jesus. The last times are near, but have not yet arrived.

If we accept as a provisional definition of eschatology the statement that the future is of primary importance and that the end of this age is rapidly approaching, there can be little doubt that Q is overwhelmingly concerned with the future and how it affects the thought and life of the community. To establish this point, the major eschatological features of Q will be documented.

1. The Son of Man is mentioned nine times in Q. As noted above, there is a complete absence of any suffering sayings. There are six future sayings:

(a) Lk. 17:24 (Mt. 24:27)

"For as the lightning flashes and lights up the sky from one side to the other, so will the Son of man be in his day."

(b) Lk. 17:26 (Mt. 24:37–39)

"As it was in the days of Noah, so will it be in the days of the Son of man. They ate, they drank, they married, they were given in marriage, until the day when Noah entered the ark, and the flood came and destroyed them all."

(c) Lk. 17:28 (Mt. 24:37–39)

"Likewise as it was in the days of Lot—they ate, they drank, they bought, they sold, they planted, they built, but on the day when Lot went out from Sodom fire and brimstone rained from heaven and destroyed them all—so will it be on the day when the Son of man is revealed."

(d) Lk. 11:30 (Mt. 12:40)

"For as Jonah became a sign to the men of Nineveh, so will the Son of man be to this generation."

---

21. Paul Hoffmann, *Studien zur Theologie der Logienquelle*, Neutestamentliche Abhandlungen, n.f. 8 (Münster: Aschendorff, 1972), pp. 34–49.

(e) Lk. 12:40 (Mt. 24:44)

"You also must be ready; for the Son of man is coming at an hour you do not expect."

(f) Lk. 12:8–9 (Mt. 10:32–33)

"And I tell you, every one who acknowledges me before men, the Son of man also will acknowledge before the angels of God; but he who denies me before men will be denied before the angels of God."

There are three present-activity sayings:

(a) Lk. 7:34 (Mt. 11:19)

"The Son of man has come eating and drinking; and you say, 'Behold, a glutton and a drunkard, a friend of tax collectors and sinners!' "

(b) Lk. 12:10 (Mt. 12:32)

"And every one who speaks a word against the Son of man will be forgiven; but he who blasphemes against the Holy Spirit will not be forgiven."

(c) Lk. 9:58 (Mt. 8:20)

And Jesus said to him, "Foxes have holes, and birds of the air have nests; but the Son of man has nowhere to lay his head."

In the light of the present analysis of the Son of Man title, we must be impressed by its frequency in Q. Through its use of this title the community expresses its concern for the role which Jesus will play in the future. The heavy concentration on judgment is consistent with other factors in the material. The present situation is primarily a time of preparation.

2. A different kind of evidence, and one which carries more weight, is the community's use of a specific eschatological form—the *Satz heiligen Rechts.*[22] It is found throughout the New Testament as well as in Q.

---

22. Ernst Käsemann,"Sentences of Holy Law in the New Testament," in *New Testament Questions of Today*, trans. W. J. Montague (Philadelphia: Fortress Press, 1969).

Lk. 12:8–9 (Mt. 10:32–33)
"And I tell you, everyone who acknowledges me before men, the Son of man also will acknowledge before the angels of God; but he who denies me before men will be denied before the angels of God."

Käsemann calls this statement a type of eschatological *lex talionis* in which the act of judging is placed in the future rather than in the present. It implies that the significance of one's current action is of utmost importance. The eschatological activity of the "judge—Son of Man" is the key to understanding one's present.

3. Another eschatological form is similar to the previous one. The eschatological correlative[23] is found only in Q in the synoptic tradition:

Lk. 11:30 (Mt. 12:40)
"For as Jonah became a sign to the men of Nineveh, so will the Son of man be to this generation."

Lk. 17:24 (Mt. 24:27)
"For as the lightning flashes and lights up the sky from one side to the other, so will the Son of man be in his day."

Lk. 17:26 (Mt. 24:37)
"As it was in the days of Noah so will it be in the days of the Son of man."

Lk. 17:28–30 (Mt. 24:38–39)
"Likewise, as it was in the days of Lot [Matthew: Noah]—they ate, they drank, they bought, they sold, they planted, they built, but on the day when Lot went out from Sodom fire and brimstone rained from heaven and destroyed them all—so will it be on the day when the Son of man is revealed."

Once again we have a judgment saying which consistently looks forward to the future—and again with the Son of Man title in a prominent position.

The character of the Q eschatology is one which stresses the tribulation about to appear. Q contains an abundance of warning and judgment sayings. In this respect, Jesus and John the Baptist in Q have very similar messages. However, Jesus' message goes beyond

---

23. R. A. Edwards, "The Eschatological Correlative as a *Gattung* in the New Testament" *ZNW* 60 (1969); 9–20.

the threat to emphasize the positive side of the judgment—the promise.

4. Proverbs are normally considered short, aphoristic statements which summarize a crucial insight into the nature of the world based upon an acute sensitivity to one's experience. Yet in Q the eschatological perspective has produced a re-construction of conventional wisdom style. When a restructuring of conventional traditions is found, as is the case with wisdom in Q, it affords an opportunity to uncover the real interests of the community. The significance attached to any statement of a general truth depends upon the stance of the hearer.[24] Given the eschatological interest of Q, particularly the imminent appearance of the Son of Man as judge, so-called gnomic statements gain new and different meaning. For example:

> Lk. 6:31 (Mt. 7:12)
> "And as you wish that men would do to you, do so to them."

> Lk. 6:38 (Mt. 7:2)
> "Give, and it will be given to you; good measure, pressed down, shaken together, running over, will be put into your lap. For the measure you give will be the measure you get back."

> Lk. 16:13 (Mt. 6:24)
> "No servant can serve two masters; for either he will hate the one and love the other, or he will be devoted to the one and despise the other. You cannot serve God and mammon."

> Lk. 11:23 (Mt. 12:30)
> "He who is not with me is against me, and he who does not gather with me scatters."

Another way in which we can illustrate the impact of the eschatological orientation upon proverbial material is to note the way in which the device of contrast is developed in Q. As all teachers know, contrast can be an effective way of highlighting an issue; to further explain what *is*, one can state what *is not*. From the point of view of those who train others in the ways of the world, this contrast technique has the added usefulness of clarifying those precise actions

---

24. The subject of wisdom will be considered further in the next chapter. For a general statement of the character of wisdom in the New Testament see W. A. Beardslee, *Literary Criticism of the New Testament,* Guides to Biblical Scholarship (Philadelphia: Fortress Press, 1970), pp. 30–41.

which are *not* acceptable as well as simply offering positive advice. When this method of presenting material is used by those who announce that the end is near, that which was *un*usual might now be the most appropriate mode of action. If the world has been turned upside down, then the unusual could become the accepted. For example:

> Lk. 6:30 (Mt. 5:42)
> "Give to everyone who begs from you; and of him who takes away your goods do not ask them again."

> Lk. 17:33 (Mt. 10:39)
> "Whoever seeks to gain his life will lose it, but whoever loses his life will preserve it."

> Lk. 9:60 (Mt. 18:22)
> "Leave the dead to bury their own dead; but as for you, go and proclaim the kingdom of God."

The community which used the Q material was definitely anticipating the arrival of Jesus as Son of Man in the near future. This eschatological orientation is *the* one most distinguishing feature of their theology. It overshadows and influences everything that they say and do. However, this community is not interested in apocalyptic speculation, as one might expect. And thus it is necessary to look at the material itself to discover just how the eschatological consciousness is expressed.

There is nothing comparable to the so-called synoptic apocalypse found in Mark 13 or the apocalyptic speculation found in 1 Thess. 4:13–5:11. As will be argued later, this lack of speculation about the end (as well as the lack of speculation about the nature of wisdom) underlies the practical, this-worldly immediacy of this community's theology. Their expectation of an imminent end has led to a careful consideration of those actions required of the faithful in the present—the time before the end. As a result, it will be necessary to look at each pericope (in Chapter VI) to discover just how this eschatological consciousness is integrated with the other themes present in the material.

IV

PROPHECY IN Q

Prophecy and wisdom are commonly recognized as two distinct literary and theological traditions within Judaism. Starting from the fact of the division of the Canon (TANAK), it was argued that the law was preserved and maintained by the priests, that the direct message of YHWH was presented (usually in poetic form) by the prophets, while the wisdom of the world was preserved by sages or wise men. The discovery of wisdom sayings which are similar to Israelite literature in other contemporary cultures has emphasized the commonality and secular nature (or roots) of the wisdom movement.[1] In the ancient world young men who deserved training and a practical education were taught the ways of the court, or society as a whole, by memorizing the practical precepts of the wise men. "Clan instructional wisdom" is now recognized as a probable origin for many wisdom sayings.[2] Each clan supplied the fundamental education of its new members and developed a functional school in which the young were acquainted with the insight and wisdom of its leaders and great teachers. The prophet, however, was considered a tool of YHWH through whom a message or announcement could

---

1. A useful survey of the development of research on wisdom literature is by R. B. Y. Scott, "The Study of Wisdom Literature," *Interpretation* 24 (1970): 20–45. The most important recent analysis of wisdom is by G. von Rad, *Wisdom in Israel* (Nashville: Abingdon Press, 1972).
2. See especially H. W. Wolff, *Amos the Prophet* (Philadelphia: Fortress Press, 1973) and his bibliography.

be presented. If the prophet himself contributed to the message it was simply a matter of clarifying the original pronouncement.[3]

Although this is a highly simplified picture, it does highlight the crucial distinction. In a religious community in which a personal God is presupposed, the ambiguity of many lessons from nature, as well as changes in the social-cultural context, will be quite visible. The continuity and immediacy of YHWH's demands are focused by the prophet, who, because of his inspiration, stands above all other sources of understanding. Why then does any wisdom material achieve canonical status? If wisdom is a distillation of experience, the context of Israel's experience (the world) is the work of YHWH. In this way, wisdom widens its concerns and summarizes the full experience of the Israelite who is influenced by YHWH. Or, put another way, wisdom is desecularized when its scope is widened to include more than the world of nature and interaction within human society. From an Israelite perspective, experience must include the impact of the divine upon the world and its influence among the actions of men.

It must be remembered, however, that the emphasis of the wisdom movement is "explanation"—working from a variety of experiences toward a principle or unifying concept. The prophet announces —the wise man synthesizes and explains. In some ways, the wisdom movement could be called a more scientific approach which operates on the assumption that there are basic laws or standards which can be discovered and stated and in which one can place his confidence. A practical, experimental attitude is present in the wisdom movement. There is an assumption about the reliability of conclusions— provided one can accurately assess the data of experience. Action in the future can be more secure and less risky. The wise man explains what he has learned from the past while the prophet announces that which YHWH has revealed. It would not be difficult for the sage to assume that the continuity which he discovers in the world is the result of YHWH's activity as creator. One would assume that the world is founded on certain basic principles. Nevertheless, these

3. C. W. Westermann, *Basic Forms of Prophetic Speech* (Philadelphia: Westminster Press, 1967). Also G. Fohrer, *Introduction to the Old Testament* (Nashville: Abingdon Press, 1965), pp. 342–362.

principles are "discovered" by the wise man when he coordinates his experience or when he recognizes that the proverbs and sayings of the sages of the past "put it all together." The wise man's insight is not considered the result of inspiration, but is the result of the ordering of the experience of the learner. In contemporary parlance, the response "right on" (meaning: I, too, can make sense of what I know in the same way) reflects a similar attitude.

A word of caution is necessary, however. We must not assume that the system is closed. Fresh insight is always a possibility not only because experience continues to add new information but also because YHWH continues to act in the world.

With these basic considerations as a starting point, we have the task in this chapter to examine carefully the Q material for prophetic attitudes. But because prophecy and wisdom are not mutually exclusive, we will eventually be required to examine each pericope.

Because our method suggests that we look for themes and ways of speaking as clues to the nature of the Q community, we note several dimensions to the elements of prophecy in Q.

1. The prophets are mentioned in five major pericopes in Q. In four of these sayings, it is explicitly stated that the prophets are those who are persecuted or dealt with violently.

(a) Lk. 6:22–23 (Mt. 5:11–12)

> "Blessed are you when men hate you, and when they exclude you and revile you, and cast out your name as evil, on account of the Son of man! Rejoice in that day, and leap for joy, for behold, your reward is great in heaven, for so their fathers did to the prophets."

(b) Lk. 7:26, 16:16 (Mt. 11:9, 11:12–13)

> "What then did you go out to see? A prophet? Yes, I tell you, and more than a prophet."
> "The law and the prophets were until John; since then the good news of the kingdom of God is preached, and every one enters it violently."

(c) Lk. 11:47–51 (Mt. 23:29–32, 34–36)

> "Woe to you! for you build the tombs of the prophets whom your fathers killed. So you are witnesses and consent to the deeds of your

fathers; for they killed them, and you build their tombs. Therefore also the Wisdom of God said, 'I will send them prophets and apostles, some of whom they will kill and persecute,' that the blood of all prophets, shed from the foundation of the world, may be required of this generation, from the blood of Abel to the blood of Zechariah, who perished between the altar and the sanctuary. Yes, I will tell you, it shall be required of this generation."

(d) Lk. 13:34–35 (Mt. 23:37–39)

"O Jerusalem, Jerusalem, killing the prophets and stoning those who are sent to you! How often would I have gathered your children together as a hen gathers her brood under her wings, and you would not! Behold, your house is forsaken! And I tell you, you will not see me until you say, 'Blessed be he who comes in the name of the Lord.' "

In a fifth passage prophets are mentioned as those who desired to see and hear what is now occurring but were unable to do so.

(e) Lk. 10:23–24 (Mt. 13:16–17)

Then turning to the disciples he said privately, "Blessed are the eyes which see what you see! For I tell you that many prophets and kings desired to see what you see, and did not see it, and to hear what you hear, and did not hear it."

The consistency of Q's attitude toward the prophets is significant. Those prophetic messengers who have in the past been the primary visible symbols of the activity of God among men are here declared to be those who also had to suffer. Q seems to assume that in its new situation the same violence of persecution is often instituted by "fathers," those respected leaders of the community who are supposed to represent the best aspects of the faith. Throughout Q we will meet this same attitude of judgment and condemnation toward the "fathers" or "this generation." In contrast, of course, there are those who have the insight to recognize the authority and purpose of Jesus and his followers. Their reward for following the true prophet is persecution and violence, just as the earlier prophets were persecuted. In this sense the Q community's attitude is quite similar to that of other elitist groups in first-century Palestine with their apocalyptic understanding of the present situation.

2. A consistent characteristic of prophetic speech is the refrain which explains the origin of a pronouncement: Thus says YHWH. A similar phrase occurs in Q. The phrase "[truly] I say to you" appears quite often. It is obviously an indication of the source of authority. However it is not merely a prophetic index, but also shows some similarity to apocalyptic idiom.[4] "I say to you" is not a true parallel to the Old Testament phrase—we would expect "Jesus said," etc. However, if the community already acknowledges the authority of the human speaker as a true prophet (who is indeed inspired by the Lord), then a simple "I say to you" would mean that the speaker does not speak on his own but rather under the influence of inspiration.

Thus, the similarity and dissimilarity of the phrase, in relation to the Old Testament forms and the apocalyptic traditions, confirms the prophetic character of the Q community.

"[Truly] I say to you" appears at every level of the synoptic tradition, though, as one might expect, more often in the material which emphasizes the sayings of Jesus. Matthew uses it fifty-seven times, Luke forty-eight times, and Mark nineteen times. A significant number (fourteen) of these occurrences in Matthew and Luke come from Q. In addition, Luke uses it nine times in a Q context where Matthew does not have it, and Matthew uses it seven times in a Q context where Luke does not have it.

Matthew	Luke
14 in Q	14 in Q
7 in a Q context	9 in a Q context
11 from Mk.	9 from Mk.
6 in a Markan context	1 in a Markan context
19 in M material	15 in L material

Although these are far from obvious statistics, we are justified in assuming that for the Q community this was certainly an important phrase although it was not uniquely theirs.

It is important to understand the implications of this prophetic

4. K. Berger, *Die Amen-Worte Jesu*, BZNW 39 (Berlin: Walter de Gruyter, 1970), esp. pp. 20–27.

refrain as it relates to the problem of the source of the Q material. If there are prophets in the Q community who are inspired to speak in Jesus' name, the words of such a prophet could be considered to be the words of Jesus, not the mere words of a human disciple. As time passes, the sayings of the "historical" Jesus could be combined with the sayings of the risen Lord which were spoken through a prophet. As a result, both sayings would be repeated by the community as sayings of Jesus which should be remembered and heeded. Our twentieth-century distinction between the "historical" Jesus and a "prophetic disciple" could easily be a meaningless (even perverse) "splitting of hairs" to the Q community.

Since our purpose is to understand Q rather than uncover sayings of the historical Jesus, there is no need to follow this line of analysis further.[5] It seems clear that there is prophetic activity in the Q community.

3. Prophetic sayings have the quality of announcement or proclamation—as opposed to a wisdom saying which draws a conclusion from a series of experiences. Statements which have a revelatory emphasis can thus be considered prophetic.

(a) Lk. 7:22 (Mt. 11:4–5)

> And he answered them, "Go and tell John what you have seen and heard: the blind receive their sight, the lame walk, lepers are cleansed, and the deaf hear, the dead are raised up, the poor have good news preached to them."

(b) Lk. 10:9 (Mt. 10:7)

> "And say to them, 'The Kingdom of God has come near to you.' "

(c) Lk. 10:12 (Mt. 10:15)

> "I tell you, it shall be more tolerable on that day for Sodom than for that town."

(d) Lk. 10:14–15 (Mt. 11:22–23)

> "But it shall be more tolerable in the judgment for Tyre and Sidon than for you. And you, Capernaum, will you be exalted to heaven? You shall be brought down to Hades."

5. T. W. Manson, *The Teaching of Jesus* (Cambridge: Cambridge University Press, 1963), p. 207. J. Jeremias, *New Testament Theology I, The Proclamation of Jesus* (New York: Charles Scribner's Sons, 1971), pp. 35–36. Cf. also Berger, *Amen-Worte.*

(e) Lk. 11:31–32 (Mt. 12:41–42)

"The queen of the South will arise at the judgment with the men of this generation and condemn them; for she came from the ends of the earth to hear the wisdom of Solomon, and behold, something greater than Solomon is here. The men of Nineveh will arise at the judgment with this generation and condemn it; for they repented at the preaching of Jonah, and behold, something greater than Jonah is here."

(f) Lk. 13:35 (Mt. 23:38–39)

"Behold, your house is forsaken! And I tell you, you will not see me until you say, 'Blessed be he who comes in the name of the Lord!' "

(g) Lk. 22:30 (Mt. 13:28)

". . . that you may eat and drink at my table in my kingdom, and sit on thrones judging the twelve tribes of Israel."

The relative scarcity of prophetic-announcement statements in Q is in part the result of the tendency in the Q material to combine prophetic sayings with wisdom sayings. The interaction of these two tendencies will be illustrated below in the next chapter.

4. Judgment sayings are considered the heart of the traditional prophetic message. The prophet is one who speaks YHWH's word to his own time in such a way as to arouse the interest, concern, and passion of the listener. It is the prophet's task to convey YHWH's reaction to the contemporary scene—usually in a negative sense. Westermann's analysis of the prophetic form of speech is based upon the primacy of the judgment motif.[6]

Closely related to the judgment saying is the warning statement which we will consider here in the same basic category.

Specific references to judgment:

Lk. 3:7 (Mt. 3:7) He said therefore to the multitudes that came out to be baptized by him, "You brood of vipers! Who warned you to flee from the wrath to come?"

Lk. 6:22 (Mt. 5:11) "Blessed are you when men hate you, and cast out your name as evil, on account of the Son of man!"

6. Westermann, *Basic Forms.*

Lk. 6:37 (Mt. 7:1–2) "Judge not, and you will not be judged; condemn not, and you will not be condemned; forgive, and you will be forgiven. . . ."

Lk. 10:9 (Mt. 10:7) ". . . heal the sick in it and say to them, 'The kingdom of God has come near to you.' "

Lk. 10:12 (Mt. 10:15) "I tell you, it shall be more tolerable on that day for Sodom than for that town "

Lk. 10:13–15 (Mt. 11:20–24) "Woe to you, Chorazin! woe to you, Bethsaida! for if the mighty works done in you had been done in Tyre and Sidon, they would have repented long ago, sitting in sackcloth and ashes. But it shall be more tolerable in the judgment for Tyre and Sidon than for you. And you, Capernaum, will you be exalted to heaven? You shall be brought down to Hades."

Lk. 11:31–32 (Mt. 12:41–42) "The queen of the South will arise at the Judgment with the men of this generation and condemn them; for she came from the ends of the earth to hear the wisdom of Solomon, and behold, something greater than Solomon is here. The men of Nineveh will arise at the judgment with this generation and condemn it; for they repented at the preaching of Jonah, and behold, something greater than Jonah is here."

Lk. 12:40 (Mt. 24:44) "You also must be ready; for the Son of man is coming at an hour you do not expect."

Lk. 22:30 (Mt. 19:28) ". . . you may eat and drink at my table in my kingdom, and sit on thrones judging the twelve tribes of Israel."

There are warnings which assume a future judgment:

Lk. 6:42 (Mt. 7:4) "Or how can you say to your brother, 'Brother, let me take out the speck that is in your eye,' when you yourself do not see the log that is in your own eye? You hypocrite, first take the log out of your own eye, and then you will see clearly to take out the speck that is in your brother's eye."

Lk. 11:39 (Mt. 23:25) And the Lord said to him, "Now you Pharisees cleanse the outside of the cup and of the dish, but inside you are full of extortion and wickedness."

Lk. 11:42 (Mt. 23:23) "But woe to you Pharisees! for you tithe mint and rue and every herb, and neglect justice and the love of God; these you ought to have done without neglecting the others."

Luke 11:47 (Mt. 23:29–30) "Woe to you! for you build the tombs of the prophets whom your fathers killed."

Lk. 11:49–52 (Mt. 23:34–36, 13) "Therefore also the wisdom of God said, 'I will send them prophets and apostles, some of whom they will kill and persecute, from the blood of Abel to the blood of Zechariah, who perished between the altar and sanctuary. Yes, I tell you, it shall be required of this generation. Woe to you lawyers! For you have taken away the key of knowledge; you did not enter yourselves, and you hindered those who were entering'"

Lk. 12:2–4 (Mt. 10:26–28) "Nothing is covered up that will not be revealed, or hidden that will not be known. Whatever you have said in the dark shall be heard in the light, and what you have whispered in private rooms shall be proclaimed upon the housetops.
"I tell you, my friends, do not fear those who kill the body, and after that have no more that they can do."

Lk. 12:8–9 (Mt. 10:32–33) "And I tell you, every one who acknowledges me before men, the Son of man also will acknowledge before the angels of God; but he who denies me before men will be denied before the angels of God."

Lk. 12:56 (Mt. 16:3) "You hypocrites! You know how to interpret the appearance of earth and sky; but why do you not know how to interpret the present time?"

Lk. 12:59 (Mt. 5:26) "I tell you, you will never get out till you have paid the very last copper."

Lk. 13:27–29 (Mt. 7:23; 8:11–12) "But he will say, 'I tell you, I do not know where you come from; depart from me, all you workers of iniquity!' There you will weep and gnash your teeth when you see Abraham and Isaac and Jacob and all the prophets in the kingdom of God and you yourselves thrust out. And men will come from east and west, and from north and south, and sit at table in the kingdom of God."

Lk. 14:26–27 (Mt. 10:37) "If any one come to me and does not hate his own father and mother and wife and children and brothers and sisters, yes, and even his own life, he cannot be my disciple."

Lk. 16:13 (Mt. 6:24) "No servant can serve two masters; for either he will hate the one and love the other, or he will be devoted to the one and despise the other. You cannot serve God and mammon."

Lk. 16:16–17 (Mt. 11:12–13) "The law and the prophets were until John; since then the good news of the kingdom of God is preached and every one enters it violently. But it is easier for heaven and earth to pass away, than for one dot of the law to become void."

Lk. 17:1 (Mt. 18:7) And he said to his disciples, "Temptations to sin are sure to come; but woe to him by whom they come!"

Lk. 17:33 (Mt. 10:39) "Whoever seeks to gain his life will lose it, but whoever loses his life will preserve it."

Lk. 17:35 (Mt. 24:41) "There will be two women grinding together; one will be taken and the other left."

Lk. 17:37 (Mt. 24:28) And they said to him, "Where, Lord?" He said to them, "Where the body is, there the eagles will be gathered together."

Lk. 19:26 (Mt. 25:29) " 'I tell you, that to every one who has will more be given; but from him who has not, even what he has will be taken away.' "

More specific judgmental images can be found:

Lk. 3:9 (Mt. 3:10) "Even now the axe is laid to the root of the trees; every tree therefore that does not bear good fruit is cut down and thrown into the fire."

Lk. 3:17 (Mt. 3:12) "His winnowing fork is in his hand, to clear his threshing floor, and to gather the wheat into his granary, but the chaff he will burn with unquenchable fire."

Lk. 6:44 (Mt. 7:16) ". . . for each tree is known by its own fruit. For figs are not gathered from thorns, nor are grapes picked from a bramble bush."

Lk. 6:49 (Mt. 7:26–27) "But he who hears and does not do them is like a man who built a house on the ground without a foundation; against which the stream broke, and immediately it fell, and the ruin of that house was great."

Lk. 10:3 (Mt. 10:16) "Go your way; behold, I send you out as lambs in the midst of wolves."

Lk. 11:24–26 (Mt. 12:43–45) "When the unclean spirit has gone out of a man, he passes through waterless places seeking rest; and finding none he says, 'I will return to my house from which I came.' And when he comes he finds it swept and put in order. Then he goes and brings seven other spirits more evil than himself, and they enter and dwell there; and the last state of that man becomes worse than the first."

Lk. 11:42–46 (Mt. 23:23, 6–7, 27–28, 4) "But woe to you Pharisees! for you tithe mint and rue and every herb, and neglect justice and the love of God; these you ought to have done without neglecting the others. Woe to you Pharisees! for you love the best seats in synagogues and salutations in the market places. Woe to you! for you are like graves which are not seen, men walk over them without knowing it."

One of the lawyers answered him, "Teacher, in saying this you reproach us also." And he said, "Woe to you lawyers also! for you load men with burdens hard to bear, and you yourselves do not touch the burdens with one of your fingers."

Lk. 14:34–35 (Mt. 5:13) "Salt is good; but if salt has lost its taste, how shall its saltness be restored? It is fit neither for the land nor for the dunghill; men throw it away. He who has ears to hear, let him hear."

Lk. 17:24 (Mt. 24:27) "For as the lightning flashes and lights up the sky from one side to the other, so will the Son of man be in his day."

Lk. 17:26–27 (Mt. 24:37–39a) "As it was in the days of Noah, so will it be in the days of the Son of man. They ate, they drank, they married, they were given in marriage, until the day when Noah entered the ark, and the flood came and destroyed them all."

Lk. 17:30 (Mt. 24:39b) ". . . so will it be on the day when the Son of man is revealed."

Lk. 19:24 (Mt. 25:28) "And he said to those who stood by, 'Take the pound from him, and give it to him who has the ten pounds.' "

5. A further indication of the interest of the Q community in prophecy is the attention given to John the Baptist. John is important in Q because he is the one who announces YHWH's message prior to the appearance of the Son of Man. The baptizing activity of John is insignificant compared to the stress placed upon his preaching. He seems to function as an example of prophecy prior to the appearance of Jesus as the Son of Man.

> Lk. 3:7–9 (Mt. 3:7–10) He said therefore to the multitudes that came out to be baptized by him, "You brood of vipers! Who warned you to flee from the wrath to come? Bear fruits that befit repentance, and do not begin to say to yourselves, 'We have Abraham as our father'; for I tell you, God is able from these stones to raise up children to Abraham. Even now the axe is laid to the root of the trees; every tree therefore that does not bear good fruit is cut down and thrown into the fire."

> Lk. 3:16–17 (Mt. 3:11–12) John answered them all, "I baptize you with water; but he who is mightier than I is coming, the thong of whose sandals I am not worthy to untie; he will baptize you with the Holy Spirit and with fire. His winnowing fork is in his hand, to clear his threshing floor, and to gather the wheat into his granary, but the chaff he will burn with unquenchable fire."

> Lk. 7:18–19 (Mt. 11:2–3) The disciples of John told him of all these things. And John, calling to him two of his disciples, sent them to the Lord, saying, "Are you he who is to come, or shall we look for another?"

> Lk. 7:22–23 (Mt. 11:4–6) And he answered them, "Go and tell John what you have seen and heard: the blind receive their sight, the lame walk, lepers are cleansed, and the deaf hear, the dead are raised up, the poor have good news preached to them. And blessed is he who takes no offense at me!"

When Q reports the confrontation between Jesus and the disciples of John, John is already in prison. Thus John has suffered the fate of all prophets—he has been persecuted and will soon be destroyed because of the incisiveness of his message. The image of the prophet in Q is consistent in the emphasis on persecution.

6. A final indication of Q's interest in the prophets is to be found in Q's use of sources from the Old Testament.

(Mic. 6:8) Lk. 11:42 (Mt. 23:23) "But woe to you Pharisees! for you tithe mint and rue and every herb, and neglect justice and the love of God; these you ought to have done without neglecting the others."

(Isa. 14:13ff) Lk. 10:15 (Mt. 11:23) "And you, Capernaum, will you be exalted to heaven? You shall be brought down to Hades."

(Isa. 14:13ff) Lk. 13:27 (Mt. 7:23) "But he will say, 'I tell you, I do not know where you come from; depart from me, all you workers of iniquity!' "

(Isa. 14:13ff) Lk. 13:29 (Mt. 8:11) "And men will come from east and west, and from north and south, and sit at table in the kingdom of God."

(Mal. 1) Lk. 7:27 (Mt. 11:10) "This is he of whom it is written, 'Behold, I send my messenger before thy face, who shall prepare thy way before thee.' "

(Isa. 29:18–19) Lk. 7:22 (Mt. 11:4–5) And he answered them, "Go and tell John what you have seen and heard: the blind receive their sight, the lame walk, lepers are cleansed, and the deaf hear, the dead are raised up, the poor have good news preached to them."

(Ps. 118:26) Lk. 13:35 (Mt. 23:38–39) "Behold, your house is forsaken! And I tell you, you will not see me until you say, 'Blessed be he who comes in the name of the Lord.' "

(Dan. 4:18ff) Lk. 13:19 (Mt. 13:31–32) "It is like a grain of mustard seed which a man took and sowed in his garden; and it grew and became a tree, and the birds of the air made nests in its branches."

(Mic. 7:6) Lk. 12:53 (Mt. 10:35–36) ". . . they will be divided, father against son and son against father, mother against daughter and daughter against her mother, mother-in-law against her daughter-in-law and daughter-in-law against her mother-in-law."

The evidence presented in this chapter is intended to show that prophecy is the second of the major themes present in the Q material. The data suggests that this community was interested in prophecy and prophets not only as a subject of speculation but also because they had reason to view themselves (or some of their fellow members) as participants in prophetic activity. Of special interest is the fact that Jesus is the source of inspiration and that the repetition of his statements makes one susceptible to his fate.

However, because these sayings are the central feature in the life of the community, their character as both prophecy and wisdom demands that the wisdom dimension, long neglected in New Testament studies, be introduced before each pericope is studied independently.

V

WISDOM IN Q

In looking for the evidence of a wisdom influence within the Q material, we will follow the procedure used in the previous chapter on prophecy.

The word "wisdom" or "wise man" is found three times in Q.

> Lk. 7:35 (Mt. 11:19b) "Yet wisdom is justified by all her children."

> Lk. 11:31 (Mt. 12:42) "The queen of the South will rise at the judgment with the men of this generation and condemn them; for she came from the ends of the earth to hear the wisdom of Solomon, and behold, something greater than Solomon is here."

> Lk. 10:21–22 (Mt. 11:25–26) In that same hour he rejoiced in the Holy Spirit and said, "I thank thee, Father, Lord of heaven and earth, that thou hast hidden these things from the wise and understanding and revealed them to babes; yea, Father, for such was thy gracious will. All things have been delivered to me by my Father; and no one knows who the Son is except the Father, or who the Father is except the Son and any one to whom the Son chooses to reveal him."

In a fourth passage, Luke refers to "the Wisdom of God" while Matthew has a simple first person pronoun "I."

> Lk. 11:49 (Mt. 23:34) "Therefore also the Wisdom of God said, 'I will send them prophets and apostles, some of whom they will kill and persecute. . . .'"

In a fifth passage, the word wisdom does not appear but the passage has often been identified as a typical wisdom saying.[1]

> Lk. 13:34–35 (Mt. 23:37–39) "O Jerusalem, Jerusalem, killing the prophets and stoning those who are sent to you! How often would I have gathered your children together as a hen gathers her brood under her wings, and you would not! Behold, your house is forsaken! And I tell you, you will not see me until you say, 'Blessed be he who comes in the name of the Lord!' "

There is little evidence of a speculative wisdom myth as the background for these sayings. Suggs has argued that it is a tendency which was developed by Matthew.[2] But we must look at the rest of the Q material before we can come to any conclusion.

In the Judaism of the three centuries preceding the rise of Christianity, the significance and scope of the wisdom movement had grown considerably. It was suggested that the law was mediated through the wisdom of God. The sending of prophets and wise men is an action of the wisdom of God—to work toward the enlightenment of men. Wisdom is said to have been the agent of creation. Nevertheless, this side of the wisdom movement is not a major aspect of Q.

The critical analysis of wisdom literature is in the process of being revised. The traditional distinction between a proverb, as the form of "folk" wisdom, and an aphorism, an artistic saying consciously composed by an educated literary class, can no longer be maintained.[3] Rather, we might make a distinction between a sentence (or saying) and an admonition. A saying is a statement registering a conclusion which grows out of experience. An admonition goes beyond a saying by asking directly for obedience. Very often, a motive clause is appended as a basis for heeding the admonition.

This distinction between sentence and admonition is a useful step toward a classification of wisdom literature and is a factor in the

---

1. For example, Felix Christ, *Jesus Sophia, Die Sophia-Christologie bei den Synoptikern*, ATANT 57 (Zürich: Zwingli Verlag, 1970), pp. 136–145.
2. M. J. Suggs, *Wisdom, Christology and Law in Matthew's Gospel* (Cambridge, Mass.: Harvard University Press, 1970), esp. pp. 63–71.
3. R. E. Murphy: "Form Criticism and Wisdom Literature," *CBQ* 31 (1969): pp. 475–483.

analysis which follows. However, the influence of a wisdom approach to life goes well beyond these forms and will be considered later.

Aphoristic sayings (sentences) in Luke (Matthew)

6:40 (10:24–5) #5	"A disciple is not above his teacher (but) . . . will be like his teacher."
6:45 (12:35) #6	"The good man out of the good treasure . . . and the evil. . . . "
7:35 (11:19c) #10	"Yet wisdom is justified by all her children (deeds)."
10:3 (10:16) #13	". . . I send you out as lambs (sheep) in the midst of wolves."
10:7 (10:10b) #13	". . . for the laborer is worthy of his wages (food). . . . "
11:10 (7:8) #18	"For every one who asks, receives, and he who seeks, finds, and to him who knocks, it will be opened."
12:2 (10:26) #24	"Nothing is covered up that will not be revealed, or hidden that will not be known."
12:6 (10:29) #24	"Are not five (two) sparrows sold for two (a) pennies (penny)?"
12:25 (6:27) #27	"And which of you by being anxious can add a cubit to his span of life?"
12:30 (6:32) #27	"For all the nations seek these things; and your Father knows you need them."
12:34 (6:21) #28	"For where your treasure is, there will your heart be also."
12:59 (5:26) #32	". . . you will never get out till you have paid the very last copper (penny)."
17:37 (24:28) #46	". . . Where the body is, there the eagles will be gathered together."
19:26 (25:29) #47	". . . every one who has will more be given; but from him who has not, even what he has will be taken away."

Admonition

The admonition moves beyond the sentence by advising that a specific action is recommended. The argument is similarly based, however; experience has taught certain lessons.

6:31 (7:12) #4	"And (whatever) as you wish that men would do to you, do so to them."
6:37 (7:1) #5	"Judge not, and you will not be judged. . . ."
10:2 (9:37) #13	"The harvest is plentiful, but the laborers are few; pray therefore the Lord of the harvest to send out laborers into his harvest."
11:9 (7:7) #18	". . . Ask and it will be given you, seek and you will find, knock and it will be opened to you."
12:7 (10:30–31) #24	"Why, even the hairs of your head are all numbered. Fear not; you are of more value than many sparrows."
12:22–23 (6:25) #27	". . . do not be anxious about your life, what you shall eat, nor about your body, what you shall put on. For life is more than food, and the body more than clothing."
12:31 (6:33) #27	"Instead, seek his kingdom and these things shall be yours as well."
12:40 (24:44) #29	"You also must be ready, for the Son of man is coming at an hour you do not expect."

Beatitude and Woe

These two forms should be understood as complements—the positive and negative aspects of a situation. There has been a continuing discussion about whether they should be considered prophetic because an announcement is being made which *could* be a divine judgment or pronouncement. However, because there is an assumption of a basic point of view about the consequences of an act or state of existence, it is possible to recognize the experience-based orientation of a wisdom saying as its primary characteristic. The beatitudes of Q, as with other New Testament beatitudes, have a formal structure which is unlike the beatitudes of the Old Testament and Apocryphal literature.[4]

Their inclusion here is based on the wisdom approach demonstrated within them. An act, life style, or situation will have its appropriate results and these results are placed within the usual eschatological context.

#3 BEATITUDES

Mt. 5:3–6

(3) "Blessed are the poor in spirit, for theirs is the kingdom of heaven,

(4) "Blessed are those who mourn, for they shall be comforted.

(5) "Blessed are the meek, for they shall inherit the earth.

(6) "Blessed are those who hunger and thirst for righteousness, for they shall be satisfied."

Lk. 6:20b–21

(20b) "Blessed are you poor, for yours is the kingdom of God.

(21) "Blessed are you that hunger now, for you shall be satisfied.

"Blessed are you that weep now, for you shall laugh."

In these two Q beatitudes the thrust is prophetic. The blessedness of those designated resides in the fact that the Kingdom of God will, in the future, establish certain priorities which are not now in effect —the poor and the hungry will not be poor and hungry then. This fact is simply stated—not argued—and none of the elaborate wisdom forms are used; rather, a situation is simply announced as a fact of the end-time—as a message from God.

Nonetheless, the simple dialectic style of the wisdom sentence is certainly present. Traditionally the sentence states a situation or condition which is easily recognized by the hearer. The speaker is doing nothing more than drawing attention to the fact that this is indeed the case—bringing to the surface the latent understanding which anyone would acknowledge were it pointed out to him.

Thus we have an interesting combination of factors—a wisdom statement about a condition of the future. The contrast between the now and then implies that the present world's criteria of worth will be overthrown. The speaker seems to have two roles (as traditionally

4. William A. Beardslee, *Literary Criticism of the New Testament*, Guides to Biblical Scholarship (Philadelphia: Fortress Press, 1970), pp. 36–39.

defined)—that of a prophet (messenger or revealer) and that of a teacher or wise man.

Mt. 5:11–12

(11) "Blessed are you when men revile you and persecute you and utter all kinds of evil against you falsely on my account. (12) Rejoice and be glad, for your reward is great in heaven; for so men persecuted the prophets who were before you."

Lk. 6:22–23

(22) "Blessed are you when men hate you, and when they exclude you and revile you, and cast out your name as evil, on account of the Son of man! (23) Rejoice in that day, and leap for joy, for behold, your reward is great in heaven; for so their fathers did to the prophets."

The situation in this beatitude is more complex. The second person pronoun (you) is added and is followed by a temporal clause (when . . .) as though those addressed are not always in a state of being reviled; they either have been and/or can expect to be in the future.

Secondly, the results of this condition are then stated more explicitly. The "reward" is not detailed but it will be in heaven, in the future kingdom. The addition of "rejoice" makes this beatitude more like the admonition in which a teacher not only states a situation and implies an approximate response, but additionally states the response which he feels is required, in this case "rejoicing." The sense of a revealed message is still present, as in the previous two examples, because the usual response to reviling is not rejoicing; this is a message which goes against normal human experience.

However, the last clause is similar to a wisdom style of argument in that it seeks to show that there is a similar situation in the past which can help to clarify the present statement. The prophets of the past had been similarly mistreated by their contemporaries who are the fathers or ancestors of the present revilers. This use of examples is not exclusively a wisdom style of argument but is quite prevalent in wisdom literature. The phrase "for thus" is also found in the eschatological correlative; there, it is followed by a future verb; here, however, by the past tense.

The reference to the prophets as prototypes has already been noted as a crucial factor in understanding the way the Q community sees its task. The implication is that this is a community which defines itself in terms of the role of a prophet.

#9 JOHN'S QUESTION AND JESUS' ANSWER

Mt. 11:2–6

(2) Now when John heard in prison about the deeds of the Christ, he sent word by his disciples. (3) and said to him, "Are you he who is to come, or shall we look for another?" (4) And Jesus answered them, "Go and tell John what you hear and see: (5) the blind receive their sight and the lame walk, lepers are cleansed and the deaf hear, and the dead are raised up, and the poor have good news preached to them. (6) And blessed is he who takes no offense at me."

Lk. 7:18–23

(18) The disciples of John told him of all these things. (19) And John, calling to him two of his disciples, sent them to the Lord, saying, "Are you he who is to come, or shall we look for another?" (20) And when the men had come to him, they said, "John the Baptist has sent us to you, saying, 'Are you he who is to come, or shall we look for another?' " (21) In that hour he cured many of diseases and plagues and evil spirits, and on many that were blind he bestowed sight. (22) And he answered them, "Go and tell John what you have seen and heard: the blind receive their sight, the lame walk, lepers are cleansed, and the deaf hear, the dead are raised up, the poor have good news preached to them. (23) And blessed is he who takes no offense at me."

The concluding beatitude is unique in making use of the conditional relative construction within the saying itself. This fact alone might indicate that it is closer to the wisdom style than the prophetic.[5]

Without the context, there is no eschatological emphasis here; it is a simple declarative which asserts that the acceptance of Jesus in the present is the condition for being blessed. The prophetic or revelatory character of this verse is contained in the implication that one's attitude toward Jesus will affect his relation with God. The condition of being blessed depends on one's taking no offense toward Jesus and is reminiscent of the *Satz heiligen Rechts* and its straightforward way of presenting the significance of Jesus.

Mt. 13:16–17

(16) "But blessed are your eyes, for they see, and your ears, for they hear. (17) Truly, I say to you, many prophets

Lk. 10:23–24

(23) Then turning to the disciples he said privately, "Blessed are the eyes which see what you see! (24) For I tell

5. Cf. K. Berger, *Die Amen-Worte Jesu,* BZNW 39 (Berlin: Walter de Gruyter, 1970).

| and righteous men longed to see what you see, and did not see it, and to hear what you hear, and did not hear it." | you that many prophets and kings desired to see what you see, and did not see it, and to hear what you hear, and did not hear it." |

This beatitude is similar to 6:22–23 in that a longer explanation is offered (verse 24 in Luke). The simple statement that is common to Matthew and Luke in verse 23 ("Blessed are the eyes which see . . .") could be quite clear at the time of its use when all those who are present are in touch with the immediate context, but it is enigmatic at any distance from the event. Thus the explanation is appended.

Verse 24 opens with the prophetic introduction which is discussed below. The explanation contrasts important figures of the past, and their unfulfilled desires to see the coming of God's agent, with the fortune of the hearers who are present at such a momentous time. The singling out of the prophets is startling and shows again the self-consciousness this community has of living within the prophetic tradition. It is not possible to reconstruct the second part of the comparison; Luke says "king," Matthew says "righteous ones."

The repetitious style of the explanation is reminiscent of the wisdom material. In this situation, we have an attempt to make people realize the gravity of the time in which they live; to draw attention to what is happening before their eyes and to what is being said in their presence.

The implied warning about the dangers of being casual is emphasized by contrasting the great-ones of the past with those who live in the present. But living in the present isn't enough—there must be a conscious understanding of *how* the present is significant. In a sense, this is the wisdom movement's basic advice (observe carefully and learn) but with the added eschatological emphasis; this "last" time is more revealing than any previous time.

| *Mt. 24:45–47* | *Lk. 12:42–44* |
| (45) "Who then is the faithful and wise servant, whom his master has set over his household, to give them their food at the proper time? (46) Blessed is that servant whom his master when he comes will find so doing. (47) | (42) And the Lord said, "Who then is the faithful and wise steward, whom his master will set over his household, to give them their portion of food at the proper time? (43) Blessed is that servant whom his master when he |

Truly, I say to you, he will set him over all his possessions."

comes will find so doing. (44) Truly I tell you, he will set him over all his possessions."

This beatitude is part of an apparent collection of material built around the householder-servant theme. 12:42 asks about the definition of the faithful and wise servant. Not only do we have the juxtaposition of faithful and wise to indicate the wisdom background of the material, but we also have the basic metaphor expanded into a parable (12:45–46). The eschatological emphasis is clearly defined in the anticipated but unannounced coming of the master.

The didactic sequence is also significant: (a) from a question about how to identify a wise and faithful servant, to (b) a beatitude which defines him as one who is constantly prepared, to (c) a pronouncement which indicates the future reward given by the master, to (d) a final statement of the whole issue in the form of a parable which tells the story now in a negative sense—an illustration of the un-wise and faithless servant.

Structurally this beatitude is unique in that the decisive event (the coming of the Lord) is placed in the middle of the description of being blessed.

The secondary character of the beatitude is evident in that the two parts of 12:43 are included as part of the whole parable complex. That is, this beatitude cannot stand on its own (as can the beatitudes in 6:20 and 6:22–23). The servant is blessed because he is in charge of all the master's possessions, not because he is to inherit the Kingdom or be accepted by the coming Lord (Son of Man).

Thus 12:43 and 44 are very similar to a wisdom admonition form. A condition is stated and the appropriate way of acting is explicitly named, not merely implied.

Once again we have a beatitude closely followed by a prophetic introductory statement (I say to you).

#36 LAMENT OVER JERUSALEM

Mt. 23:37–39

(37) "O Jerusalem, Jerusalem, killing the prophets and stoning those who are

Lk. 13:34–35

(34) "O Jerusalem, Jerusalem, killing the prophets and stoning those who are

sent to you! How often would I have gathered your children together as a hen gathers her brood under her wings, and you would not! (38) Behold, your house is forsaken and desolate. (39) For I tell you, you will not see me again, until you say, 'Blessed is he who comes in the name of the Lord.' "	sent to you. How often would I have gathered your children together as a hen gathers her brood under her wings, and you would not! (35) Behold, your house is forsaken. And I tell you, you will not see me until you say, 'Blessed is he who comes in the name of the Lord.' "

The situation in this pericope is reversed—the beatitude is the conclusion of a statement introduced by the "I say to you" phrase. Thus, within the context, the beatitude is completely secondary although it could have existed on its own in some other context.

The opening is a typical prophetic judgment pronouncement which assumes that YHWH speaks merely to make clear his judgment. This is followed by the prophetic introductory phrase.

Taking verses 34 and 35 together, the beatitude must refer to those people who are the new prophets, those who come now in Jesus' name and are accepted just as the prophets of old were rejected. The beatitude is the content of the advice so that the entire section functions as a warning or admonition.

Once again we have a unique situation: the beatitude is that which one should say, it is not an independent statement. The one who is blessed is the one who addresses the listener (the Q community prophet?). The *recognition of the legitimacy* of the Q community prophet will result in the Lord becoming viable to these people.

In 13:34–35 there is a combination of prophetic and wisdom traditions, forms, and themes. The prophets are mentioned as the ones who have suffered at the hands of the people; there is a prophetic introduction (I say to you) to the conclusion and its content as well as the implication that the newcomers are the new prophets. Wisdom influence is present in the lament and the specific image of the hen protecting its young.

The woe is found in both prophetic and wisdom literature and its point of origin is still disputed. Nonetheless, the wisdom characteristics of the woe permit us to assume that it can be adapted to serve the purpose of the sage.

In Q, the woe appears in six different places. Whether the four woes of Luke's Sermon on the Plain (6:24–26) were originally part of Q or not will not concern us here.

#14 WOES ON GALILEE

Mt. 11:20–24

(20) Then he began to upbraid the cities where most of his mighty works had been done, because they did not repent. (21) "Woe to you, Chorazin! woe to you, Bethsaida! for if the mighty works done in you had been done in Tyre and Sidon, they would have repented long ago in sackcloth and ashes. (22) But I tell you, it shall be more tolerable on the day of judgment for Tyre and Sidon than for you. (23) And you, Capernaum, will you be exalted to Heaven? You shall be brought down to Hades. For if the mighty works done in you had been done in Sodom, it would have remained until this day. (24) But I tell you that it shall be more tolerable on the day of judgment for the land of Sodom than for you."

Lk. 10:13–15

(13) "Woe to you, Chorazin! woe to you, Bethsaida! for if the mighty works done in you had been done in Tyre and Sidon, they would have repented long ago, sitting in sackcloth and ashes. (14) But it shall be more tolerable in the judgment for Tyre and Sidon than for you. (15) And you, Capernaum, will you be exalted to heaven? You shall be brought down to Hades."

Lk. 10:12

(12) "I tell you it shall be more tolerable on that day for Sodom than for that town."

Chorazin and Bethsaida are compared unfavorably with the Gentile cities of Tyre and Sidon. The actions which should have initiated repentance *have* taken place. Thus the woe simply states a condition which already exists—even though the actual punishment has not yet taken place. Both the emphasis on comparison and the use of the woe to verbalize an already established fact (rather than to warn in advance) point to the wisdom background.

The purpose for stating this lamentable situation is, of course, to warn others to avoid putting themselves in the same condition. And the material which follows (10:14–15) continues the comparison between cities, but now explicitly states that the judgment is the real concern of the community. 10:14 is a prophetic addition tacked onto the end of the woe to clarify its significance to the hearer—the prophet *knows* that it will be easier for Tyre and Sidon in the judgment. 10:15 introduces another Galilean town, Capernaum, and announces that this town will be sent to Hades, not raised up to heaven at the judgment.

It might be useful to make a distinction between a prophetic and a wisdom threat. The implied warning in the woe-saying itself (wisdom threat) is expanded and clarified with the prophetic threats that follow it.

Mt. 23:23	*Lk. 11:42*
(23) "Woe to you, scribes and Pharisees, hypocrites! for you tithe mint and dill and cummin, and have neglected the weightier matters of the law, justice and mercy and faith; these you ought to have done, without neglecting the others."	(42) "But woe to you Pharisees! for you tithe mint and rue and every herb, and neglect justice and the love of God; these you ought to have done, without neglecting the others."

Again we have "woe" followed by the dative personal pronoun and then the name of those to whom the woe is addressed. The explanation in this example (and in the next four) follows immediately, introduced by "for."

The condition which demands the lament is the neglect of the wider concerns and the excessive concentration on minutiae. As in the previous woe, the condition is one which already exists, the Pharisees are criticized because of the actions they have already performed.

The basic emphasis here is prophetic because the entire saying functions as a message which reveals God's priorities, priorities which have been violated by the Pharisees.

Mt. 23:27–28	*Lk. 11:44*
(17) "Woe to you, scribes and Pharisees, hypocrites! for you are like whitewashed tombs, which outwardly appear beautiful, but within they are full of dead men's bones and all uncleanness. (18) So you also outwardly appear righteous to men, but within you are full of hypocrisy and iniquity."	(44) "Woe to you! for you are like graves which are not seen, and men walk over them without knowing it."

All that we can reconstruct in this verse is the woe form ("woe" and a personal pronoun in the dative case with an introductory "for"). Both versions mention tombs or graves and the deceptiveness of them but the points being made are quite different.

Mt. 23:29–31	*Lk. 11:47*
(29) "Woe to you, scribes and Pharisees, hypocrites! for you build the tombs of the prophets and adorn the monuments of the righteous, (30) saying, 'If we had lived in the days of our fathers, we would not have taken part with them in shedding the blood of the prophets.' (31) Thus you witness against yourselves, that you are sons of those who murdered the prophets."	(47) "Woe to you! for you build the tombs of the prophets whom your fathers killed."

The "woe" introduction and the "for" clause appear again. Matthew's version is much longer but there is enough agreement to suggest that the Pharisees are criticized for appearing to be what they are not. The wisdom emphasis is quite prevalent here: the sons acknowledge the evil deeds of the fathers by building tombs to the prophets in an effort to overcome the stain of the past, but they have not learned to see the activity of the contemporary prophets, Jesus and his followers. Experience should lead to enlightenment about the present, not merely to an acknowledgment of the mistakes of others. The Pharisees have therefore violated the basic principle of the wisdom movement.

Mt. 23:13	*Lk. 11:52*
(13) "But woe to you, scribes and Pharisees, hypocrites! because you shut the kingdom of heaven against men; for you neither enter yourselves, nor allow those who would enter to go in."	(52) "Woe to you lawyers! for you have taken away the key of knowledge; you did not enter yourselves, and you hindered those who were entering."

There has been considerable rewriting in this saying by Matthew or Luke. What remain besides the basic form ("woe to you" and "for") doubles the responsibility of the Pharisees. Not only have they failed to learn the lesson of the past, but they also keep others from entering the Kingdom of God.

#43 WARNING AGAINST OFFENSES

Mt. 18:6–7	*Mk. 9:42*	*Lk. 17:1–3a*
(6) "But whoever causes one of these little ones who believe in me to sin, it would be better for him to have a great millstone fastened round his neck and to be drowned in the depth of the sea. (7) "Woe to the world for temptations to sin! For it is necessary that temptations come, but woe to the man by whom the temptation comes!"	(42) "Whoever causes one of these little ones who believe in me to sin, it would be better for him if a great millstone were hung round his neck and he were thrown into the sea."	(1) And he said to his disciples, "Temptations to sin are sure to come; but woe to him by whom they come! (2) It would be better for him if a millstone were hung round his neck and he were cast into the sea, than that he should cause one of these little ones to sin. (3a) Take heed to yourselves. . . ."

In this pericope we are dealing with both Mark and Q. Matthew and Luke have incorporated a Q woe into the Markan material and what remains of Q is minimal. Luke does not have any dative pronoun or noun, while Matthew has "to the man." There is no "for" clause because the woe itself is a way of completing the idea already stated. Because of the fragmentary nature of the evidence for Q, and because of the lack of the usual form, it is not possible to say anything definite about Q.

Comparison Sayings

The distinction between prophetic and wisdom sayings assumes the time-honored division between (a) prophetic statements based on revelation from an authority beyond the prophet and (b) wisdom statements based on revelation of experience in the world. The prophet appeals to YHWH's authority to give emphasis to his words, while the sage appeals to the evidence contained in either common, everyday experience or the collected experience of the past. In either case, the sage appeals to evidence in a way the prophet does not.

However, the minute such an assertion is stated, it is necessary to pause and admit that the prophet does appeal to experience—and uses evidence—about past occurrences and in reference to current events, customs, and circumstances. The increasing evidence of a wisdom influence in the prophetic books makes it clear that this distinction needs further elaboration and testing.[6] There is little hesitancy among scholars to talk about wisdom literature, but not much precision when it comes to a definition. The form-critical distinction between a sentence and an admonition holds some promise but does not cover all of the material usually labeled wisdom.

If these form-critical categories are unable to describe adequately the full complexity of the situation, it is tempting to say that we are again confronted with the "form vs. content" problem—not in the sense of an either/or, however, but in the sense of an interaction of one with the other.

In this study of the Q material, two kinds of instruction or ways of teaching have become apparent. The term "way" must be understood here to be a combination of the form of presentation and the rationale behind it that gives it life. It seems best to maintain the distinction between wisdom instruction and prophetic instruction. Both ways could make use of the sentence form or the admonition, while implying that the source of the authority for such a saying is either experience or revelation. In addition, we must recognize that in the wisdom movement revelation can be confirmed or explained by an appeal to experience; the way of things in God's world could corroborate the statements of the prophets. Part of the content of experience is the reality of God's influence in the world. Or, to put it another way, the order which the wise man finds in the world (as he reflects on his experience) is not the result of happenstance, but is founded upon the fact that the world is God's creation.

A tendency to look for wisdom, or prophecy, or law—based on an analysis of Old Testament material—could cause us to overlook the peculiar way these "traditions" have evolved by the time we reach the 1st century A.D. For example, the close connection between wisdom and Torah in Sirach has often been noted. The tendency for earlier "traditions" to combine or interact and, as a result, lose their

---

6. H. W. Wolff, *Amos the Prophet* (Philadelphia: Fortress Press, 1973); J. Lindblom, "Wisdom in the Old Testament Prophets" in *Wisdom in Israel and in the Ancient Near East*, VT Supplements 3 (Leiden: Brill, 1955), pp. 192–204. J. W. Whedbee, *Isaiah and Wisdom* (Nashville: Abingdon, 1971).

definite boundaries, therefore, raises the question: if wisdom influence is a factor in the development of Q, how does one identify it? What specifically can we point to as an example of wisdom influence?

An answer to this question can be suggested by a consideration of the comparison saying. In an attempt to characterize the nature of the wisdom approach to life von Rad suggests that the primary point at issue is the relation between an act and its consequence.[7] This basic orientation of the wise man is expressed primarily through an appeal to experience, i.e., by stating similar situations or examples and perhaps also stating the nature of the connection (with "like," "as," etc.). But when we ask how this attitude is expressed in a literary context, we find that the literary technique of juxtaposing statements is used to imply a relationship which the teacher feels can be grasped by the hearer. The hearer is forced to reach for the conclusion, he must participate in the "lesson," if any teaching-learning is to take place. There are times, of course, when the sage will not merely juxtapose statements, but will draw an explicit conclusion using the admonition form. It is more common, however, to find that he implies his conclusion by the juxtaposition of statements.

I have called this method of instruction a "comparison." In Q, there are three related items: (1) explicit comparatives, (2) parables, and (3) suggested or implied comparisons. These literary types are indicative of the general attitude of the Q community. Thus, to argue for a wisdom influence in Q, we must look for more than basic structural forms (as sentences or admonitions). The new situation of this community has forced a combination of eschatology, wisdom, and prophecy which will not fit the boundaries established by the study of Old Testament literature.

In its widest sense, then, the phenomenon of "comparison" is the placing of statements side-by-side in order to encourage the hearer (reader) to see a relationship which the speaker assumes is there and which he also assumes the hearer will be able to comprehend. It is a didactic method which forces an involvement of the hearer. However, it can achieve nothing but bafflement if the hearer does not comprehend the basic, fundamental experiences which are part of

---

7. G. von Rad, *Wisdom in Israel* (Nashville: Abingdon Press, 1972), pp. 124–137.

the experience of the teacher. If that common foundation is present, the overall effect of the method can be quite powerful.

The most obvious and subtle expression of this method of teaching is the parable. There is little that can be added here to the vast literature on the parable. Its character as extended metaphor and its "sometime" introduction containing a simile both reflect a didactic method which relies on the juxtaposition of common experience with either an idea, concept, or experience needing clarification.[8] There are times, of course, when the second element of the juxtaposition is not obvious and we are left with the difficult problem of finding an appropriate interpretation. (In Q, such an example is the parable of the "unclean spirit.") But within the parable itself, two "ways," attitudes, or items are juxtaposed. Examples are:

> wheat and chaff in the threshing parable of John (#1)
> the mote and the log in the eye (#5)
> the house on rock or sand (#5)
> two activities of the children in the market place (#10)
> places of rest for animals vs. the Son of Man's restlessness (#12)
> "before" and "after" conditions in the parable of the unclean spirit (#20)
> light and darkness in the parable of the eye (#22)
> the householder (prepared and unprepared) (#29)
> the good or bad servant (#29)
> "before" and "after" in the parables of the mustard seed and leaven (#33 and #34)
> those who accept and those who refuse to attend the great banquet (#37)
> the lost sheep and the 99 (#40)
> the use and misuse of talents (#47)

Not only the parable itself, but the structure within the parable illustrates this technique of comparison or juxtaposition.

The second type of saying is the comparative. In this construction a juxtaposition of items is related in a hierarchial way—more than, greater than, less than, etc. The appeal to experience is based on a

8. Cf. especially Amos N. Wilder, *The Language of the Gospel: Early Christian Rhetoric* (New York: Harper & Row, 1964), pp. 79–96; Robert Funk, *Language, Hermeneutic and Word of God* (New York: Harper & Row, 1966), pp. 136–162; Dan O. Via, *The Parables* (Philadelphia: Fortress Press, 1967). Norman Perrin, "The Modern Interpretation of the Parables of Jesus and the Problem of Hermeneutics," *Interpretation* 25 (1971): 131–148.

general statement followed by the expansion or intensification of the first part of the saying.

The effectiveness of such a device is well-known to any teacher. If one can attract attention (and perhaps assent) for a general statement, then the move to a comparative will heighten the point.

In Q, comparatives are used in different contexts: (a) to contrast the present with the past *or* future:

> a greater than Solomon is here (#21)
> a greater than Jonah is here (#21)
> Sodom more tolerable than that city (#13)
> more tolerable for Tyre and Sidon in the judgment than for you (#14)
> the last state of that man is worse than the first (unclean spirit) (#20);

(b) to contrast the degree or position of an item:

> John is more than a prophet, he is greater than any human but less than the least-one in the Kingdom (#10)
> how much more will the father give good gifts if you do (#18)
> life is more than food, the body is more than clothing, you are of more value, than they (#27).

The third kind of comparison or juxtaposition is that area in which we are close to a parable but not actually there. It is often a matter of individual judgment whether these sayings are to be considered parables or not. The point being made is conveyed by some juxtaposition. In its simplest form are these examples:

6:31 (Mt. 7:12) #4	Golden Rule ("And as you wish men to do to you, do so to them.")
6:37 (Mt. 7:1–2) #5	"Judge not, and you will not be judged. . . ."
6:43 (Mt. 7:18) #6	". . . For a bad tree [does not produce] good fruit."
6:44 (Mt. 7:16) #6	"For figs are not gathered from thorns. . . ."

6:45 (Mt. 12:35) #6	"The good man out of the good treasure . . . produces good, and the man out of the evil treasure produces evil."
10:7 (Mt. 10:10) #13	". . . for the laborer deserves his wages (food). . . ."
12:24 (Mt. 6:26) #27	"[Ravens] neither sow nor reap."

Any one of these statements could form the basis for a parable. Either as simple statements or as admonitions, instruction is conveyed by an emphasis on the act-consequence relationship by using some form of doubleness.

There are some explicit similes and correlatives:

6:36 (Mt. 5:48) #4	"Be merciful, as even your Father is merciful."
6:40 (Mt. 10:24–25) #5	"A disciple is not above his teacher . . . like his teacher."
10:3 (Mt. 10:16) #13	". . . behold, I send you as lambs in the midst of the wolves."
11:30 (Mt. 12:40) #21	"For as Jonah [was] . . . so will the Son of man be. . . ."
13:34 (Mt. 23:37) #36	". . . as a hen gathers her brood under her wings. . . ."
17:6 (Mt. 17:20) #45	". . . as a grain of mustard seed."
17:26 (Mt. 24:27) #46	"As . . . in the days of Noah so . . . in the days of the Son of man."

In this group, then, a particular form of juxtaposing (the simile) is used and the character of the relationship is made explicit.

Finally, there are more elaborate juxtapositions:

7:8 (Mt. 8:9) #8	[Centurion's statement] ". . . I say to one, 'Go,' and he goes; . . . 'Come,' . . . 'Do this,' . . ."

10:2 (Mt. 9:37–38) #13	". . . The harvest is plentiful, but the laborers are few; pray, therefore, the Lord of the harvest to send out laborers into his harvest."
10:16 (Mt. 10:40) #15	"He who hears you hears me, and he who rejects you, rejects me, and he who rejects me rejects him who sent me."
11:13 (Mt. 7:11) #18	"If you then, who are evil, know how to give good gifts to your children, how much more will the heavenly Father give the Holy Spirit to those who ask him!"
12:6 (Mt. 10:29) #24	Are not five sparrows sold for two pennies? And not one of them is forgotten. . . ."
12:27–30 (Mt. 6:28–32) #27	"Consider the lilies, how . . . neither toil nor spin . . . if God so clothes the grass which is alive today and tomorrow is thrown into the oven, . . . more . . . you. O men of little faith. . . . For all the nations . . . seek these things . . . your Father knows that you need them."
12:33–34 (Mt. 6:19–21) #28	". . . treasure . . . in the heavens . . . where no thief . . . no moth. . . . For where your treasure is, there will your heart be also."
16:13 (Mt. 6:24) #41	"No servant can serve two masters; for. . . ."

These examples illustrate a tendency or attitude which is not explained by the application of regular form-critical analysis. The term "comparison" is really too limiting a term and juxtaposition doesn't say enough. "Comparison" seems to imply a specific, expounded, spelled-out, explicit relationship which is not always present in these sayings. "Juxtaposition" is literally correct but does not emphasize the full context or the assumptions which are present. "Wisdom instruction" seems to be the best term because it differentiates between the prophetic announcement and the appeal to the world—and it does not necessarily reject an acknowledgment of God's activity in the continuation of order in the world.[9]

Defined in this way, a very definite wisdom influence occurs in the Q sayings. If such an influence does exist, what difference does it make? It has been argued that any talk about "wisdom influence" has meaning if it is understood as a way of arguing, or better, of establishing the authority for a particular point of view or conclusion. The existence of such an influence in Q is important, therefore, in an attempt to reconstruct the theology of a community which collects sayings of Jesus. In addition to the eschatology and prophecy in Q, we must consider the influence of wisdom. This peculiar combination of eschatology, wisdom, and prophecy—with very little concern for the saving effect of Jesus's death—must be recognized in the reconstruction of the theology.

Jesus' sayings are the source of true wisdom; because the appearance of the Son of Man is imminent, the immediate future, before the end, is of crucial significance. In order to survive the judgment, when he returns, the members of this community have collected the sayings of the judge as a guide for living in these last days. There is no need to speculate on the significance of his death—all prophets suffer at the hands of the religious establishment.

The problem of the Q community is thus a practical one—living righteously in the last days. Discipleship is their primary interest. What better guide to this time than the words of the judge himself?

Wisdom instruction emphasizes the practical. The disciple is taught (instructed) by reference to the way of things in the world. But it is a world in which experience must be modified by the new understanding, that is, that the Kingdom is at hand. Thus, a basically prophetic statement is developed in a wisdom context. Knowing that the end is imminent allows or even demands a fuller comprehension of the lessons of experience.

Wisdom and eschatology may seem to be an unusual combination. As a literary expression, however, comparison/juxtaposition is a fitting way to express an eschatological awareness. Anticipation of

---

9. This point is emphasized by von Rad, *Wisdom*, esp. pp. 109–110.

the end—i.e., being in the last days—assumes that there are signs and indications at hand and that a full recognition of present circumstances must prevail. Because a time of change is imminent, attention must be focused on the "last days." By comparing or juxtaposing experience within the context of the imminent, expected change, the full implications of the new situation can be communicated. This leads in the direction of apocalyptic even if no specific, developed apocalyptic speculation exists in Q.

VI

THE INTERACTION OF THEMES IN Q

If all of these isolated components are to contribute to an understanding of Q, they must be shown to be interwoven effectively and not merely lumped together. It has been presumed throughout this study that there is a unity lying behind the variety—not simply the unity of a *kerygma* (in Dodd's sense of the term) but an inherent rationale. The interaction of the themes already isolated must be illustrated with the data itself before a final conclusion is drawn.

This is not a commentary in which every aspect or difficulty is discussed. Rather, it is a survey of the Q material to highlight the issues which have been mentioned and seek to understand their interrelation.

#1 THE PREACHING OF JOHN

Mt. 3:7–10

(7) But when he saw many of the Pharisees and Sadducees coming for baptism, he said to them, "You brood of vipers! Who warned you to flee from the wrath to come? (8) Bear fruit that befits repentance, (9) and do not presume to say to yourselves, 'We have Abraham as our father'; for I tell you, God is able from these stones to raise up children to Abraham. (10) Even now the axe is laid to the root of the trees; every tree therefore that does not bear good fruit is cut down and thrown into the fire."

Lk. 3:7–9

(7) He said therefore to the multitudes that came out to be baptized by him, "You brood of vipers! Who warned you to flee from the wrath to come? (8) Bear fruits that befit repentance, and do not begin to say to yourselves, 'We have Abraham as our father'; for I tell you, God is able from these stones to raise up children to Abraham. (9) Even now the axe is laid to the root of the trees; every tree therefore that does not bear good fruit is cut down and thrown into the fire."

Mt. 3:11–12	Mk. 1:7–8	Lk. 3:15–18
(11) "I baptize you with water for repentance, but he who is coming after me is mightier than I, whose sandals I am not worthy to carry; he will baptize you with the Holy Spirit and with fire. (12) His winnowing fork is in his hand, and he will clear his threshing floor and gather his wheat into the granary, but the chaff he will burn with unquenchable fire."	(7) And he preached, saying, "After me comes he who is mightier than I, the thong of whose sandals I am not worthy to stoop down and untie. (8) I have baptized you with water; but he will baptize you with the Holy Spirit."	(15) As the people were in expectation, and all men questioned in their hearts concerning John, whether perhaps he were the Christ, (16) John answered them all, "I baptize you with water; but he who is mightier than I is coming, the thong of whose sandals I am not worthy to untie; he will baptize you with the Holy Spirit and with fire. (17) His winnowing fork is in his hand, to clear his threshing floor, and to gather the wheat into his granary, but the chaff he will burn with unquenchable fire." (18) So, with many other exhortations, he preached good news to the people.

The eschatological assumption in John's preaching is clearly stated in 3:7: "Who warned you to flee from the wrath to come?" The emphasis is obviously on the new understanding of the present ("now") and particularly the need to prepare for the judgment. The addition of the word "fire" in 3:16 picks up the judgmental reference in a specific apocalyptic image. The threshing parable (in 3:17) continues the emphasis on judgment not only with the image of fire, but also using a standard harvest image. It is significant that the final verb in the parable ("will burn" 3:17) is in the future tense.

The prophetic element is especially evident in 3:8 which combines the prophetic introduction with a declarative statement of what God is capable of doing—to raise up children to Abraham—without any appeal to experience but rather with a reference to what he has already accomplished in the past. An added prophetic characteristic is the threat and warning implicit throughout the passage. In 3:9 a prophetic parable threatens an ultimate judgment upon those who do not measure up to God's standards. 3:17 is also a prophetic judgment parable.

When one shifts perspective, however, and looks at this section from the interests of instructional wisdom, new insight results. There are no explicit classical proverbs but the two parables both use common instructional wisdom techniques, i.e., an item of common experience serves as the basis for instructing the listener about the inevitability of God's judgment. From a wisdom point of view, the parable in 3:9 is a sentence which we can call a prophetic parable because of its immediate context, especially the statement: "Even now the axe is laid to the root of the trees." The parable in 3:17 also has eschatological and prophetic overtones, but its force is heightened by the use of an item of common experience, that of the thresher and his normal response to the grain and the chaff. Both parables appeal to the usual—the normal—course of events; certain situations require an obvious response; that is a given in the experience of a culture. This experience is now used to teach the listener about a related, and in some ways similar, situation. Is it any wonder that wisdom techniques have been found in prophetic books?

#2 TEMPTATIONS

Mt. 4:1–11

(1) Then Jesus was led up by the Spirit into the wilderness to be tempted by the devil. (2) And he fasted forty days and forty nights, and afterward he was hungry. (3) And the tempter came and said to him, "If you are the Son of God, command these stones to become loaves of bread." (4) But he answered, "It is written,

'Man shall not live by bread alone,
but by every word that proceeds
from the mouth of God.' "

(5) Then the devil took him to the holy city, and set him on the pinnacle of the temple, (6) and said to him, "If you are the Son of God, throw yourself down; for it is written,

'He will give his angels charge of you,' and

Lk. 4:1–13

(1) And Jesus, full of the Holy Spirit, returned from the Jordan, and was led by the Spirit (2) for forty days in the wilderness, tempted by the devil. And he ate nothing in those days; and when they were ended, he was hungry. (3) The devil said to him, "If you are the Son of God, command this stone to become bread." (4) And Jesus answered him, "It is written, 'Man shall not live by bread alone.' " (5) And the devil took him up, and showed him all the kingdoms of the world in a moment of time, (6) and said to him, "To you I will give all this authority and their glory; for it has been delivered to me, and I give it to whom I will. (7) If you, then, will worship me, it shall all be yours." (8) And Jesus

'On their hands they will bear you up, lest you strike your foot against a stone.' "
(7) Jesus said to him, "Again it is written,
'You shall not tempt the Lord your God.' "
(8) Again, the devil took him to a very high mountain, and showed him all the kingdoms of the world and the glory of them; (9) and he said to him, "All these I will give you, if you will fall down and worship me." (10) Then Jesus said to him, "Begone, Satan! for it is written,
'You shall worship the Lord your God and him only shall you serve.' "
(11) Then the devil left him, and behold, angels came and ministered to him.

answered him, "It is written,
'You shall worship the Lord your God, and him only shall you serve.' "
(9) And he took him to Jerusalem, and set him on the pinnacle of the temple, and said to him, "If you are the Son of God, throw yourself down from here;
(10) for it is written,
'He will give his angels charge of you, to guard you,'
(11) and
'On their hands they will bear you up, lest you strike your foot against a stone.' "
(12) And Jesus answered him, "It is said, 'You shall not tempt the Lord your God.' " (13) And when the devil had ended every temptation, he departed from him until an opportune time.

This incident is truly unique in Q. It is easy to imagine a debate of this type taking place among the rabbis, with the quoting of the Old Testament by both sides. The applicability of the passage quoted is assumed and not argued, as one would expect in a Qumran-style *pesher* interpretation. Jesus quotes only from Deuteronomy in this passage, as many have pointed out.

There is nothing particularly eschatological about this passage, there are no distinctive prophetic materials or emphases, and it lacks any usual wisdom influence.

How, then, does it happen to be in Q? Many have suggested that it is either not Q at all or that it is not original Q, i.e., it was added at a later date by either a redactor of the Q material, or by the evangelists.[1]

If one considers the purpose of Q to be a guide to discipleship, this pericope could be considered more than a statement of Christology. The ability of Jesus to counter effectively the devil in this "fencing match" could be a guide to the disciple. It is consistent with the rest

1. W. Schmithals, "Kein Streit um des Kaisers Bart: Zur Diskussion über das Bekenntnis zu Jesus Christus," *Evangelische Kommentare* 3 (1970): 80; S. Schulz, *Q, Die Spruchquelle der Evangelisten* (Zürich: Theologischer Verlag, 1972), pp. 177–190.

of Q in that the emphasis is upon the sayings of Jesus rather than his actions.

#3 BEATITUDES

Mt. 5:3–12

(3) "Blessed are the poor in spirit, for theirs is the kingdom of heaven.

(4) "Blessed are those who mourn, for they shall be comforted.

(5) "Blessed are the meek, for they shall inherit the earth.

(6) "Blessed are those who hunger and thirst for righteousness, for they shall be satisfied.

(7) "Blessed are the merciful, for they shall obtain mercy.

(8) "Blessed are the pure in heart, for they shall see God.

(9) "Blessed are the peacemakers, for they shall be called sons of God.

(10) "Blessed are those who are persecuted for righteousness' sake, for theirs is the kingdom of heaven.

(11) "Blessed are you when men revile you and persecute you falsely on my account.

(12) Rejoice and be glad, for your reward is great in heaven, for so men persecuted the prophets who were before you."

Lk. 6:20b–23

(20b) "Blessed are you poor, for yours is the kingdom of God.

(21) "Blessed are you that hunger now, for you shall be satisfied.

"Blessed are you that weep now, for you shall laugh.

(22) "Blessed are you when men hate you, and when they exclude you and revile you, and cast out your name as evil, on account of the Son of Man!

(23) Rejoice in that day, and leap with joy, for behold, your reward is great in heaven; for so their fathers did to the prophets.

Lk. 6:22–23 has been considered above as part of the expanded fourth beatitude. We need only add here that the advice to rejoice is based upon the assurance that the rewards of heaven are the reverse of the persecution of the present. The guarantee of this assurance is to be found in the comparison with the earlier prophets. Thus we have here an indication of the combination of motifs which is evident throughout Q—eschatological hope, wisdom teaching about the present, and either a reference to the prophets as models and examples or the use of prophet-messenger forms of speech. The tendency to draw comparisons is an obvious feature of the wisdom movement —but in this example, it is defined by the future hope and not limited to the present.

It is possible that the final reference to the prophets has been explicitly added by the Q community. The "so" in Luke (6:23) and in Matthew (5:12), in conjunction with the word "for," is a stylistic feature of the eschatological correlative (see above) and is definitely a characteristic of the Q material.

THE WOES

Lk. 6:24–26
(24) "But woe to you that are rich, for you have received your consolation.
(25) "Woe to you that are full now, for you shall hunger.
"Woe to you that laugh now, for you shall mourn and weep.
(26) "Woe to you when all speak well of you, for so their fathers did to the false prophets."

This collection of woes is included here for comparative purposes. It may have been a part of Q but it is impossible to say because it is not found in Matthew. (See above.)

#4 LOVE OF ENEMIES

Mt. 5:38–48
(38) "You have heard that it was said. 'An eye for an eye and a tooth for a tooth.' (39) But I say to you, Do not resist one who is evil. But if any one strikes you on the right cheek, turn to him the other also; (40) and if any one would sue you and take your coat, let him have your cloak as well; (41) and if any one forces you to go one mile, go with him two miles. (42) Give to him who begs from you, and do not refuse him who would borrow from you.

(43) "You have heard that it was said, 'You shall love your neighbor and hate your enemy.' (44) But I say to you, Love your enemies and pray for those who persecute you, (45) so that you may be sons of your Father who

Lk. 6:27–36
(27) "But I say to you that hear, Love your enemies, do good to those who hate you, (28) bless those who curse you, pray for those who abuse you. (29) To him who strikes you on the cheek, offer the other also; and from him who takes away your cloak do not withhold your coat as well. (30) Give to every one who begs from you; and of him who takes away your goods do not ask them again. (31) And as you wish that men would do to you, do so to them. (32) "If you love those who love you, what credit is that to you? For even sinners love those who love them. (33) And if you do good to those who do good to you, what credit is that to you? For even sinners do the same. (34) And if you lend to those

is in heaven; for he makes his sun
rise on the evil and on the good, and
sends rain on the just and on the unjust.
(46) For if you love those who love
you, what reward have you? Do not even
the tax collectors do the same? (47)
And if you salute only your brethren,
what more are you doing than others?
Do not even the Gentiles do the same?
(48) You, therefore, must be perfect,
as your heavenly Father is perfect."

from whom you hope to receive, what
credit is that to you? Even sinners lend
to sinners, to receive as much again. (35)
But love your enemies, and do good,
and lend, expecting nothing in return;
and your reward will be great, and you
will be sons of the Most High; for he is
kind to the ungrateful and the selfish.
(36) Be merciful, even as your Father
is merciful."

[See 6:31]

Mt. 7:12
(12) "So whatever you wish that men
would do to you, do so to them; for this
is the law and the prophets."

The editorial activity of Matthew and/or Luke is quite extensive
in this section. Where precise verbal similarity is missing, however,
we do have at times similar phrases which, although they cannot be
used to reconstruct the text, do allow some filling in of the gaps.

In 6:27 and 28 the admonition to love one's enemies and to pray
for those who persecute exhibits the typical wisdom exhortation, but
seems to have reversed the normal ways of the world. This advice
is not practical (as a result of empirical, astute observation of the
ways of the world) but is understandable in the eschatological context of the imminent return of the judge. The basis for a practical
decision is built upon the future and not upon the past (the accu-
mulated tradition of careful observation). A wisdom is now available
which transcends usual advice.

Verses 29 and 30 are even more fragmentary although the gist of
the admonition is clear—turn the other cheek and offer your cloaks.
In the press of the end-time, normal precautions are meaningless.
Verse 30 is a normal kind of wisdom advice, although it can take on
added meaning in this context. Giving is now meant in a very
elaborate way: you do not need to hold back at any point, for any
purpose.

Verse 31 is the Golden Rule and has received more than its share
of attention. The simpler and less conditioned version of Luke should

be noted. The meaning is similar, however, and uses the wisdom style of giving advice: the juxtaposing of two sides. Out of context, it could be argued that this statement is based on an ego-centered ethic. But its position here forces us to reconsider its implications. The expectations of the Q community are radically different now. What they anticipate or desire from men, as they prepare for the coming of the judge, will demand a similar rethinking about what they must do to prepare for the end.

The two sentences contained in verses 32–33 also use a wisdom approach, this time with a conditional-relative structure and an implication established by the use of rhetorical questions. If we assume that the hearer will know the usual way of the world, he is encouraged to recognize the manner in which the new situation has placed a new alternative before him. No specific advice is offered. Nonetheless, it is clear that these sentences imply that appropriate action of a very specific sort is required.

This section ends with two specific admonitions in verses 35 and 36. Verse 35 is an admonition followed by a direct statement of the results, if the admonition is carried out. The use of the word "sons" as a designation of the true members of the community is consistent with other sections of Q and with the general tendency of wisdom admonitions (Listen my son, etc.). Verse 36 makes use of the comparison technique: act as your father acts. Matthew and Luke differ significantly in which quality of God is being stressed, but the form of the admonition is retained.

Throughout this pericope there is a basic assumption that the speaker is thoroughly aware both of the nature of the present situation (the imminent coming of the judge) and the quality of action which is required by the situation. In this sense, the prophetic dimension is present as an undertone or foundation for the self-understanding of the community—a self-understanding which is expressed primarily in wisdom forms as a preparation for the coming judgment.

#5 JUDGING

Mt. 7:1–5	Mk. 4:24–25	Lk. 6:37–42
(1) "Judge not, that you be not judged. (2) For with	(24) And he said to them, "Take heed what you	(37) "Judge not, and you will not be judged; condemn

the judgment you pronounce you will be judged, and the measure you give will be the measure you get. (3) Why do you see the speck that is in your brother's eye, but do not notice the log that is in your own eye? (4) Or how can you say to your brother, 'Let me take the speck out of your eye,' when there is the log in your own eye? (5) You hypocrite, first take the log out of your own eye, and then you will see clearly to take the speck out of your brother's eye."

Mt. 12:36–37
(36) "I tell you, on the day of judgment men will render account for every careless word they utter; (37) for by your words you will be justified, and by your words you will be condemned."

Mt. 15:14
(14) "Let them alone; they are blind guides. And if a blind man leads a blind man, both will fall into a pit."

Mt. 10:24–25
(24) "A disciple is not above his teacher, nor a a servant above his master; (25) it is enough for the disciple to be like his teacher, and the servant like his master. If they have called the master of the house Beelzebul, how much more will they malign those of his household."

hear; the measure you give will be the measure you get, and still more will be given you. (25) For to him who has will more be given; and from him who has not, even what he has will be taken away."

not, and you will not be condemned; forgive, and you will be forgiven; (38) give, and it will be given to you; good measure, pressed down, shaken together, running over, will be put into your lap. For the measure you give will be the measure you get back." (39) He also told them a parable: "Can a blind man lead a blind man? Will they not both fall into a pit? (40) A disciple is not above his teacher, but every one when he is fully taught will be like his teacher. (41) Why do you see the speck that is in your brother's eye, but do not notice the log that is in your own eye? (42) Or how can you say to your brother, 'Brother, let me take out the speck that is in your eye,' when you yourself do not see the log that is in your own eye? You hypocrite, first take the log out of your own eye, and then you will see clearly to take out the speck that is in your brother's eye."

[See 6:37–38]

[See 6:39]

[See 6:40]

The admonitory character of the opening saying (6:37) is obvious. However, Matthew's form of the second clause "that you be not judged" (aorist passive subjunctive) results in a gnomic saying: you should not judge because you may be judged in return. If you criticize, you are more likely to be criticized in return. This could readily be understood as a proverbial statement based on experiential wisdom. Luke, on the contrary, uses "and you will not be judged" ("*kaì ou*" with the aorist passive subjunctive), thereby giving the second half of the saying the force of the future tense: do not judge and you *will not* be judged. Thus the Lukan form heightens the admonitory aspect because it reflects the eschatological interest.

Lk. 6:39 shows significant signs of redaction, by composition, on the part of Matthew and/or Luke. Nevertheless, the basic parable remains with its wisdom implications: the blind who lead their fellow blind men are sure to fall into a pit. Luke prefers the question form, which might be an indication of an older tradition. The classic appeal to experience is used to establish a general conclusion. But we cannot be more precise about the Q application because the context in Matthew and Luke differs.

Lk. 6:40 shows how Luke develops the idea contained in the parable. This sentence must be considered on its own, however, because Matthew's placing of the saying is quite different. Not only is this sentence a typical wisdom form, its content concerns a basic wisdom situation, the relation of teacher to disciple or student. The second part of the saying cannot be reconstructed completely but the exact agreement ("like his teacher"), as well as its similar use in Matthew and Luke, indicates that the point was to warn the disciple to be patient and to persevere so that his goal of reaching the level of the teacher might some day be achieved. The result is an emphasis on discipleship as a way of achieving; by oneself, the goal cannot be attained.

Besides Matthew's more elaborate comparison (servant and lord as well as disciple and teacher) he stresses the need for humility even more than Luke, i.e., it is enough to be *like* the teacher!

Lk. 6:41–42 contains the well-known parable which again stresses the humility and self-criticism needed by the disciple—the parable of the mote and beam. Once again, it is Luke's arrangement we are following here; Matthew does not place these materials together as Luke does.

The differences between Matthew and Luke are basically stylistic and do not affect the meaning.

Exaggeration is a typical wisdom device useful in any teaching situation. Its effect here is striking because it emphasizes the necessary lack of self-criticism for any teacher or person attempting to give advice. Consistency in the application of principles is an absolute requirement if one expects others to listen to one's exhortation. The appearance of the word "hypocrite" carries the meaning of the saying that much further. Both experience and comparison are combined to make the point.

Section 5, therefore, is clearly an example of Q's interest in the usefulness of wisdom forms to achieve its goal.

#6 FRUITS

Mt. 7:15–20

(15) "Beware of false prophets, who come to you in sheep's clothing but inwardly are ravenous wolves. (16) You will know them by their fruits. Are grapes gathered from thorns, or figs from thistles? (17) So, every sound tree bears good fruit, but the bad tree bears evil fruit. (18) A sound tree cannot bear evil fruit, nor can a bad tree bear good fruit. (19) Every tree that does not bear good fruit is cut down and thrown into the fire. (20) Thus you will know them by their fruits."

Lk. 6:43–45

(43) "For no good tree bears bad fruit, nor again does a bad tree bear good fruit; (44) for each tree is known by its own fruit. For figs are not gathered from thorns, nor are grapes picked from a bramble bush. (45) The good man out of the good treasure of his heart produces good, and the evil man out of his evil treasure produces evil; for out of the abundance of the heart his mouth speaks."

Mt. 12:33–35

(33) "Either make the tree good, and its fruit good; or make the tree bad, and its fruit bad; for the tree is known by its fruit. (34) You brood of vipers! how can you speak good, when you are evil? For out of the abundance of the heart the mouth speaks. (35) The good man out of his good treasure brings forth good, and the evil man out of his evil treasure brings forth evil."

[See 6:45]

The lack of agreement between Matthew and Luke about the order of these sayings precludes any argument based on composition or arrangement and we are forced to view each section independently.

Lk. 6:43 is a sentence which, by implication, teaches the need for integrity. Drawing on an agricultural commonplace, it establishes a simple equation between the host and its fruit. We might be tempted to rephrase it as: a tree is defined as good or bad simply by its fruit.

Mt. 7:18 has made it a more forceful saying by inserting "can" in the first part of the sentence and implying it in the second. However, in Mt. 7:17 we find the same verb as Luke, which suggests that the simpler form of the statement (without can) is the original.

Lk. 6:44 is another sentence. Agreement between Matthew and Luke is clear, even though choice of vocabulary and word order differ.

The point being made is identical to that of 6:43. Whether these two sayings belong together in Q or not, they demonstrate the interest of the Q community in a reliance upon action (or obedience) as a method for determining membership among the true followers or disciples. The specific technique for elaborating the main point is again contrast. The basic statement is obviously true because experience tells one that figs are not found on thorns, etc. Note: grapes and figs appear in Matthew and Luke as the good fruit, but they agree only on thorns as images of evil (Matthew: thistle; Luke: bramble-bushes).

Lk. 6:45 is also a sentence. Luke places it immediately after the two previous verses and so it functions for him as a kind of admonition, or at least an explanatory sentence. Matthew places it in quite another context. Luke's style is more economical, but he has a concluding expansion of the image which shows that all these images are to be thought of in terms of one's speech. Matthew does not use this saying (12:34b) as a conclusion and as a result it does not have the same finality that it does in Luke.

#7 HOUSE ON ROCK

Mt. 7:21–27	*Lk. 6:46–49*
(21) "Not every one who says to me, 'Lord, Lord,' shall enter the kingdom of	(46) "Why do you call me 'Lord, Lord,' and not do what I tell you? (47)

heaven, but he who does the will of my Father who is in heaven. (22) On that day many will say to me, 'Lord, Lord, did we not prophesy in your name, and cast out demons in your name, and do many mighty works in your name?' (23) And then will I declare to them, 'I never knew you; depart from me, you evildoers.'

(24) "Every one then who hears these words of mine and does them will be like a wise man who built his house upon the rock; (25) and the rain fell, and the floods came, and the winds blew and beat upon that house, but it did not fall, because it had been founded on the rock. (26) And every one who hears these words of mine and does not do them will be like a foolish man who built his house upon the sand; (27) and the rain fell, and the floods came, and the winds blew and beat against that house, and it fell; and great was the fall of it."

Every one who comes to me and hears my words and does them, I will show you what he is like: (48) he is like a man building a house, who dug deep, and laid the foundation upon rock; and when a flood arose, the stream broke against that house and could not shake it, because it had been well built. (49) But he who hears and does not do them is like a man who built a house on the ground without a foundation; against which the stream broke, and immediately it fell, and the ruin of that house was great."

Lk. 6:46 is too fragmentary to allow one to recover the structure. The title "Lord" is shared, as is the verb "do/does." The emphasis is similar, however; the stress is on those who by their actions demonstrate their faith rather than merely announce it. Matthew has a full expansion of this theme which does not appear in Luke.

Lk. 6:47 serves to introduce the parable in 48–49 for which there is quite significant verbal agreement. The wisdom characteristics are evident—particularly in the explicit correlation between the image of the houses and the introduction which states, again, that the firm foundation is the hearing and the doing of the words of the Lord. Hearing and doing are illustrated by contrasting the two ways: (1) the positive results in 6:47–48 and (2) the negative results in 6:49. In each section there is an introduction which uses the comparison word (like) and the words for hearing and doing.

The conditional relative sentence is also significant. It is a more casuistic and less apodictic form. K. Berger has argued that is a sentence structure which is more prevalent in the wisdom literature than among the prophets.[2] It is wisdom-like in its correlation of the facts of the building trade with the basic rules or laws one should apply to men.

#8 CENTURION OF CAPERNAUM

Mt. 8:5–13

(5) As he entered Capernaum, a centurion came forward to him, beseeching him (6) and saying, "Lord, my servant is lying paralyzed at home, in terrible distress." (7) And he said to him, "I will come and heal him." (8) But the centurion answered him, "Lord, I am not worthy to have you come under my roof; but only say the word, and my servant will be healed. (9) For I am a man with authority, with soldiers under me; and I say to one, 'Go,' and he goes, and to another, 'Come,' and he comes, and to my slave, 'Do this,' and he does it." (10) When Jesus heard him, he marveled, and said to those who followed him, "Truly, I say to you, not even in Israel have I found such faith. (11) I tell you many will come from east and west and sit at table with Abraham, Isaac, and Jacob in the kingdom of heaven, (12) while sons of the kingdom will be thrown into the outer darkness; there men will weep and gnash their teeth." (13) And to the centurion Jesus said, "Go; be it done for you as you have believed." And the servant was healed at that very moment.

Lk. 7:1–10

(1) After he had ended all his sayings in the hearing of the people he entered Capernaum. (2) Now a centurion had a slave who was dear to him, who was sick and at the point of death. (3) When he heard of Jesus, he sent to him elders of the Jews, asking him to come and heal his slave. (4) And when they came to Jesus, they besought him earnestly, saying, "He is worthy to have you do this for him, (5) for he loves our nation, and built us our synagogue." (6) And Jesus went with them. When he was not far from the house, the Centurion sent friends to him, saying to him, "Lord, do not trouble yourself, for I am not worthy to have you come under my roof; (7) therefore I did not presume to come to you. But say the word, and let my servant be healed. (8) For I am a man set under authority, with soldiers under me: and I say to one, 'Go,' and he goes; and to another, 'Come,' and he comes; and to my slave, 'Do this,' and he does it." (9) When Jesus heard this he marveled at him, and turned and said to the multitude that followed him, "I tell you, not even in Israel have I found such faith." (10) And when those who had been sent returned to the house they found the slave well.

Lk. 13:28–29

(28) There you will weep and gnash your teeth, when you see Abraham and Isaac and Jacob and all the prophets in

---

2. K. Berger, *Die Amen-Worte Jesu*, BZNW 39 (Berlin: Walter de Gruyter, 1970), pp. 35–36.

[See 8:11]

the kingdom of God and you yourselves thrust out. (29) And men will come from east and west, and from north and south, and sit at table in the kingdom of God.

This passage has been repeatedly spotlighted as one of the few examples of narrative material in Q. Yet when we isolate the Q material it is only in Lk. 7:6–9 that there is any real agreement between Matthew and Luke. Verses 6–9 contain the words of the centurion, Jesus' astonishment, and his reply. Thus the supposed miracle story and narrative of Q are in fact a saying of Jesus which places his stamp of approval upon the saying of a centurion. Whether we should see this as a reflection of the structure of an apophthegm (pronouncement story), or simply say that Matthew and Luke have rewritten the narrative elements, it is impossible to say. If one considers only what is definitely Q, we are confronted not by a miracle story at all, but by a parable about the non-Israelite whose faith is illustrated in the combination of his words and deeds.

The speech of the centurion is interesting in itself, for it uses traditional wisdom arguments: the centurion shows that he understands authority by claiming and describing his position as an authoritative one. Here is a man who has learned by observation, who sees the connection between his own experience and the ways of the world. This lesson is then applied to his situation in relation to Jesus. The faith that Jesus affirms is a confidence in God's action in the world; not a supernatural intervention, but a continuing presence which guarantees the stability of things.

Jesus' pronouncement in verse 9 is a prophetic statement. It has the traditional forms and sentiments. But it is also a declaration of faith spoken by a Gentile who has not yet seen Jesus' authority confirmed by a miracle. The centurion's confidence is based on his anticipation of success, which is itself founded upon his recognition of the authority of Jesus.

#9 JOHN'S QUESTION AND JESUS' ANSWER

Mt. 11:2–6

(2) Now when John heard in prison about the deeds of the Christ, he sent

Lk. 7:18–23

(18) The disciples of John told him of all these things. (19) And John,

word by his disciples (3) and said to him, "Are you he who is to come, or shall we look for another?" (4) And Jesus answered them, "Go and tell John what you hear and see: (5) the blind receive their sight and the lame walk, lepers are cleansed and the deaf hear and the dead are raised up, and the poor have good news preached to them. (6) And blessed is he who takes no offense at me."

calling to him two of his disciples, sent them to the Lord, saying, "Are you he who is to come, or shall we look for another?" (20) And when the men had come to him, they said, "John the Baptist has sent us to you, saying, 'Are you he who is to come, or shall we look for another?'" (21) In that hour he cured many of diseases and plagues and evil spirits, and on many that were blind he bestowed sight. (22) And he answered them, "Go and tell John what you have seen and heard: the blind receive their sight, the lame walk, lepers are cleansed, and the deaf hear, the dead are raised up, the poor have good news preached to them. (23) And blessed is he who takes no offense at me."

Matthew and Luke agree in reporting the question which John the Baptist addresses to Jesus by means of his disciples: "Are you the one who is to come, or should we expect another?" The eschatological implications of this query are obvious. It is without doubt the kind of question which would be asked in the Q community: how are we to know that Jesus is "the coming one"? It is basically an appeal for validation or authentication.

Jesus' response is not a self-declaration but rather an appeal to experience. The evidence is available. It is a common wisdom response. But the activity appealed to is not typical of worldly events. The quote comes from a prophet (Isaiah) who is describing the end-time. It will be a time when God is active—and such a time has now appeared. Thus validation is based on spirit-led activity and on an appeal to the fulfillment of the inspired words of Isaiah. It is a composite quote and the climax is apparently in the unexpected conclusion: the poor have the gospel preached to them. Jesus as teacher and inspired sage is highlighted.

The concluding beatitude has been discussed above. Apparently Matthew and Luke both found it here in the Q material. Although it refers to the present, the context (especially the opening question) implies an eschatological emphasis: Jesus is the one who is yet (for the Q community) to come. Their participation in the last days is, in part, the continuation of Jesus' task of preaching to the poor.

#10 JESUS' WITNESS TO JOHN

Mt. 11:7–19

(7) As they went away, Jesus began to speak to the crowds concerning John: "What did you go out into the wilderness to behold? A reed shaken by the wind? Why then did you go out? To see a man clothed in soft raiment? Behold, those who wear soft raiment are in kings' houses. (90) Why then did you go out? To see a prophet? Yes, I tell you, and more than a prophet. (10) This is he of whom it is written,
  'Behold, I send a messenger before thy face, who shall prepare thy way before thee.'
(11) Truly, I say to you, among those born of women there has risen no one greater than John the Baptist; yet he who is least in the kingdom of heaven is greater than he. (12) From the days of John the Baptist until now the kingdom of heaven has suffered violence, and men of violence take it by force. (13) For all the prophets and the law prophesied until John; (14) and if you are willing to accept it, he is Elijah who is to come. (15) He who has ears to hear, let him hear.
(16) "But to what shall I compare this generation. It is like children sitting in the market places and calling to their playmates, (17) 'We piped to you, and you did not dance; we wailed, and you did not mourn.' (18) For John came neither eating nor drinking and they say, 'He has a demon'; (19) the Son of man came eating and drinking, and they say, 'Behold, a glutton and a drunkard, a friend of tax collectors and sinners!'" Yet wisdom is justified by her deeds."

Lk. 7:24–35

(24) When the messengers of John had gone, he began to speak to the crowds concerning John: "What did you go out into the wilderness to behold? A reed shaken by the wind? (25) What then did you go out to see? A man clothed in soft raiment? Behold, those who are gorgeously appareled and live in luxury are in kings' courts. (26) What then did you go out to see? A prophet? Yes, I tell you, and more than a prophet. (27) This is he of whom it is written.
  'Behold, I send my messenger before thy face, who shall prepare thy way before thee.'
(28) I tell you, among those born of women none is greater than John; yet he who is least in the kingdom of God is greater than he." (29) (When they heard this all the people and the tax collectors justified God, having been baptized with the baptism of John; (30) but the Pharisees and the lawyers rejected the purpose of God for themselves, not having been baptized by him.)
(31) "To what then shall I compare the men of this generation, and what are they like? (32) They are like children sitting in the market place and calling to one another,
  'We piped to you, and you did not dance; we wailed, and you did not weep.'
(33) For John the Baptist has come eating no bread and drinking no wine; and you say, 'He has a demon.' (34) The Son of man has come eating and drinking; and you say, 'Behold, a glutton and a drunkard, a friend of tax collectors and sinners!' (35) Yet wisdom is justified by all her children."

96

Mt. 21:31–32

(31) "Which of the two did the will of his father?" They said, "The first." Jesus said to them, "Truly, I say to you, the tax collectors and the harlots go into the kingdom of God before you. (32) For John came to you in the way of righteousness, and you did not believe him, but the tax collectors and the harlots believed him; and even when you saw it, you did not afterward repent and believe him."

[See 11:12–13]

[See 7:29–30]

Lk. 16:16

(16) "The law and the prophets were until John; since then the good news of the kingdom of God is preached, and everyone enters it violently."

This is a long, double collection of material with an interesting use of questions—this time not from John's disciples but rhetorical questions from Jesus.

Lk. 7:24–28 is a consistent unit. Jesus is portrayed as using a typical device to highlight the positive answer he wishes to emphasize in verse 28. Three times the question is asked: What did you go out to see? The answer each time is phrased as a question. When the question-answer is elaborated, in verse 25, the verbal parallel between Matthew and Luke breaks down. This method of piling question upon question is a standard teaching device and is indicative of the wisdom background. But the entire sequence of questions is merely introductory to two prophetic announcements which also use the word "prophet" and the prophetic-style introduction.

They went to see a prophet, but more than a prophet. The quotation from Ex. 23:30 and Mal. 3:1 defines the greatness of John by referring to his actual coming. The task he performs is to prepare the way of *the people* before *them*; he does not prepare the way for the Lord to travel, but the way of the people who must be prepared when the Lord comes.

This revelational announcement is followed by another, with the same prophetic introduction. John's role is now put in a wider context; although he is the greatest as a "preparer," he is still not one of those in the Kingdom. The present tense verb ("is") in 28b is a problem—one would expect the future tense. This particular passage has elicited a lot of comment and cannot be dealt with fully here. If this passage is seen in the context argued above for the Q community, we have here an instance in which the Q community is making a distinction between John as the one who prepared, and Jesus as the preparer who is also the judge of the future.

If John is more than a prophet, what is he? He is the one who is inspired to speak God's word in the last time. He is the final prophet who establishes the context in which Jesus can carry on his work. John died the typical prophetic death before the turn of the age when Jesus is vindicated by God by his being elevated to God's right hand as Son of Man. Verse 28 also uses the teaching device of contrasting John to those in the Kingdom, but it is accomplished by a double use of "greater" with "least" at the opening of the second clause. The phrase "greater than" is a characteristic of the Q community as we have seen.

The second half of this collection is unified by the continued reference to John the Baptist. It is composed of three typical wisdom teaching forms—the parable, a comparison sentence, and a sentence.

The parable (7:31–32) opens with a question about how this generation can be described or pictured. They are like children who are satisfied by nothing; no matter what game is suggested, they fail to respond. The application of the parable follows in the comparison/sentence—with an introductory "for." John comes as an ascetic and "you" say he is crazy; the Son of Man comes as a normal, ordinary individual and "you" criticize him for being a drunkard and a glutton! He associates with all levels of society, and "you" call him a friend of the dregs of society! The point of all this seems to be the highlighting of a problem which, if properly illuminated, can be easily seen. This is not revelation—it is a typical wisdom appeal to the facts of existence which all people can readily understand once it has been pointed out. Thus by combining two wisdom teaching devices, a major point is scored.

The conclusion substantiated this: And wisdom is justified by her children (Luke) or works (Matthew). In itself, this sentence could mean merely that you can tell what is good by its success (the good fruit comes from a good tree). But in this context, the word "wisdom" and the referent of works or children make its meaning more difficult to define. The understanding of the Q community seems to depend on the parable-sentence that preceded it. Thus, it suggests: don't assess a man by his superficial appearance. Jesus is to be judged by the effect he has on people; if he is attuned to the essence of the universe, God's creation, he will be able to act in a way which is harmonious and helpful. Being wise and being inspired are not opposites but variations on the attempt to do God's work. By implication then, Jesus and John are wisdom's children or deeds because they both do God's work, even though they undoubtedly stand at two different places or levels in God's plan of action. Thus, in Q, Jesus is not identified as the Wisdom of God, but as one who does God's work, which is being a child (or deed) of God.

Section 10 is a combination of prophetic and wisdom forms and themes. Prophet and sage are both included.

#11 COMMISSIONING THE TWELVE

Mt. 10:1	*Mk. 6:6b–13*	*Lk. 9:1–6*
(1) And he called to him his twelve disciples and gave them authority over unclean spirits, to cast them out, and to heal every disease and every infirmity.	(6b) And he went about among the villages teaching. (7) And he called to him the twelve, and began to send them out two by two, and gave them authority over the unclean spirits. (8) He charged them to take nothing for their journey except a staff; no bread, no bag, no money in their belts; (9) but to wear sandals and not put on two tunics. (10) And he said to them, "Where you enter a house, stay there until you leave the place. (11) And if any place will not receive you and they refuse to hear you, when you leave, shake off the dust that is on your feet for a testimony against them." (12) So they went out and preached that men should repent. (13) And they cast out many demons,	(1) And he called the twelve together and gave them power and authority over all demons and to cure diseases, (2) and he sent them out to preach the kingdom of God and to heal. (3) And he said to them, "Take nothing for your journey, no staff, nor bag, nor bread, nor money; and do not have two tunics. (4) And whatever house you enter, stay there, and from there depart. (5) And wherever they do not receive you, when you leave that town shake off the dust from your feet as a testimony against them." (6) And they departed and went through the villages, preaching the gospel and healing everywhere.

Mt. 10:7–11
(7) "And preach as you go, saying, 'The kingdom of heaven is at hand.' (8) Heal the sick, raise the dead, cleanse lepers, cast out demons. You received without pay, give without pay. (9) Take no gold, nor silver nor copper in your belts, (10) no bag for your journey, nor two tunics, nor sandals, nor a staff; for the laborer deserves his food. (11) And whatever town or village you enter, find out who is worthy in it, and stay with him until you depart."

Mt. 10:14	and anointed with oil many
(14) "And if any one will not receive you or listen to your words, shake off the dust from your feet as you leave that house or town."	that were sick and healed them.

| | [See 6:11] | [See 9:5] |

A clear reconstruction of Q is impossible. Much of this material is paralleled in Mark and the only significant verses for our interest are Lk. 9:1–2.

Matthew and Luke have added a phrase about the healing of the sick to the Markan context about the casting out of evil spirits. This is followed in both Matthew and Luke by a Q comment about the preaching of the Kingdom.

It is also impossible to say anything about the *form* of the material in Q because of the redaction of Matthew and Luke. We are left, then, with the apparent interest of the Q community in showing the connection of the preaching of the Kingdom with the casting out of demons and healing the sick. The fact that this is placed in the context of the commission to the disciples means that the Q community feels its task to be composed of, at least, these two activities. The basic frame of reference is the eschatological expectation with the spirit active among them to enable the healing and exorcism to occur.

The similarity between this pericope and the quotation from Isaiah 29 and 35 in section 9 (Jesus' answer to John) helps to substantiate the suggestion that the Q community sees its task as the continuation of the deeds of Jesus. They must continue his work of preaching and healing until he comes again. Only in this way will men be prepared for the judgment.

#12 ON FOLLOWING JESUS

Mt. 8:18–22	Lk. 9:57–62
(18) Now when Jesus saw great crowds around him, he gave orders to go over to the other side. (19) And a scribe came up and said to him, "Teacher, I will follow you wherever you go." (20) And Jesus said to him,	(57) As they were going along the road, a man said to him, "I will follow you wherever you go." (58) And Jesus said to him, "Foxes have holes, and birds of the air have nests; but the Son of man has nowhere to lay

"Foxes have holes, and birds of the air have nests; but the Son of man has nowhere to lay his head." (21) Another of the disciples said to him, "Lord, let me first go and bury my father." (22) But Jesus said to him, "Follow me, and leave the dead to bury their own dead."

his head." (59) To another he said, "Follow me." But he said, "Lord, let me first go and bury my father." (60) But he said to him, "Leave the dead to bury their own dead; but as for you, go and proclaim the kingdom of God." (61) Another said, "I will follow you, Lord; but let me first say farewell to those at my home." (62) Jesus said to him, "No one who puts his hand to the plow and looks back is fit for the kingdom of God."

Two apparently independent units have been placed side by side because they clarify the strenuous demands of true discipleship. In both cases the form is the same—a statement from a potential disciple followed by a response from Jesus which stresses, in a nondirect way, the pressing demands of the eschatological situation. Verbal similarity is quite complete.

Jesus replies to the "pious" assertion ("I will follow you wherever you go") with a parable-like statement which once again employs contrast as a teaching device. Without an eschatological context this would be a simple statement about the lot of the common man (son of man) in a depressed economy. But "Son of Man" also has a specific, future, judgmental meaning for the Q community. Persecution and homelessness are implied by the saying. Traditional wisdom has been transformed by eschatology from a statement about the nature of life to a warning or even a threat. The *Sitz* for this saying is probably the Q community impressing upon proselytes the harsh demands of "the Way."

The second saying contains no explicit eschatological statement. By form, it is a sentence which could refer to the need to live in the present and to "let bygones be bygones." However, in light of the previous saying *and* the saying of the disciple which it answers, it becomes a warning about the importance of the present upon those who expect the coming of the Son of Man.

#13 COMMISSIONING OF 70

Mt. 9:37–38
(37) Then he said to his disciples, "The harvest is plentiful, but the laborers

Lk. 10:1–12
(1) After this the Lord appointed seventy others, and sent them on ahead

are few; (38) pray therefore the Lord
of the harvest to send out laborers into
his harvest."

Mt. 10:7–16

(7) "And preach as you go, saying,
'The kingdom of heaven is at hand.'
(8) Heal the sick, raise the dead, cleanse
lepers, cast out demons. You received
without pay, give without pay. (9)
Take no gold, nor silver, nor copper in
your belts, (10) no bag for your
journey, nor two tunics, nor sandals, nor
a staff; for the laborer deserves
his food. (11) And whatever town or
village you enter, find out who is
worthy in it, and stay with him until
you depart. (12) As you enter the house,
salute it. (13) And if the house is
worthy, let your peace come upon it;
but if it is not worthy, let your peace
return to you. (14) And if any one will
not receive you or listen to your words,
shake off the dust from your feet as
you leave that house or town. (15)
Truly, I say to you, it shall be more
tolerable on the day of judgment for
the land of Sodom and Gomorrah
than for that town."
(16) "Behold, I send you out as
sheep in the midst of wolves; so be
wise as serpents and innocent as doves."

of him, two by two, into every town
and place where he himself was about
to come. (2) And he said to them,
"The harvest is plentiful, but the
laborers are few; pray therefore the
Lord of the harvest to send out
laborers into his harvest. (3) Go your
way; behold, I send you out as lambs
in the midst of wolves. (4) Carry
no purse, no bag, no sandals; and
salute no one on the road. (5) Whatever
house you enter, first say, 'Peace be
to this house!' (6) And if a son of peace
is there, your peace shall rest upon him;
but if not, it shall return to you. (7)
And remain in the same house, eating and
drinking what they provide, for the
laborer deserves his wages; do not go
from house to house. (8) Whenever
you enter a town and they receive
you, eat what is set before you;
(9) heal the sick in it and say to them,
'The kingdom of God has come near
to you.' (10) But whenever you enter
a town and they do not receive you, go
into its streets and say, (11) 'Even the
dust of your town that clings to
our feet, we wipe off against you;
nevertheless know this, that the kingdom of God has come near.' (12) I
tell you, it shall be more tolerable on
that day for Sodom than for that town."

Lk. 10:2 is a classic admonition form which has been modified by
an eschatological emphasis. Because the harvest is upon us (a typical
image of the end-time) and because the workers are few, one must
pray to the Lord requesting other workers. In the third reference to
harvest at the end of verse 2, the harvest is described as *his* harvest.
One senses that the time is running out, that the workers who are
presently toiling cannot accomplish their task without the added help
the Lord can supply. The overall effect is a heightening of the dedica-
tion of those at work.

Verse 3 uses another image of the end, the helplessness, the
expected trouble, and the persecution of lambs or sheep among

wolves. Although the image itself relies on the wisdom approach, the opening makes this saying a prophetic word—"Behold, I send." Once again there is an assumption in the Q community of the reality of persecution and trouble, just as the prophets have always been persecuted because of their mission (being sent to speak). The following verse (Lk. 10.4 and Mt. 10:9 10) is attached to verse 3 by both Matthew and Luke (Matthew's version being much fuller). Because the only direct parallels are the phrases "no bag" and "no sandals," the extensive redaction does not allow a reconstruction of the form. Apparently the advice about the actual requirements of the mission have changed. The same can be said for the following verse (Lk. 10:5 and Mt. 10:12) which defines the action necessary when entering a house.

Verse 6 retains the basic conditional opening and in the apodosis recommends the speaking of peace upon those people (or that house) which is receptive to the mission. This situation would be the appropriate place for a beatitude in the eschatological sense which we have seen above.

Only the second half of verse 7 is Q material and it serves as a conclusion—"for the worker is worthy of his wages" (Matthew: food). This is a typical wisdom sentence. It is not clear if the worker is thought of as the Q missionary who should expect his work to be rewarded, or if it refers to the audience which will be rewarded if they have truly responded to the message presented. Either interpretation would seem fitting.

Verses 9–12 show signs of fairly extensive redaction but enough remains to allow us to pick up the theme and to recognize that Matthew and Luke agree in keeping this material together. It is impossible to reconstruct precise forms.

Verse 9 is interesting in that it connects the healing activity of the community with the preaching of the nearness of the Kingdom. Thus we have further confirmation of the theme which appeared in the pericope about John—that the preaching is the climax of those activities of the community but that healing and exorcism are also a definite part of its life. At this point the prophetic emphasis is paramount.

Verse 10 underlines the expectation of rejection which is assumed by the Q community and verse 11 merely indicates that there was some advice about how to respond when a city or house shows no response to the mission.

Finally in verse 12 we have a Q-community conclusion which is prophetic in form and content. It has the prophetic messenger introduction and states a conclusion which is not based on common-sense analysis but which is determined by the assumptions which they already possess because of their understanding of Jesus and his future return. The eschatological intent is obvious. However, the wisdom influence is recognizable in the use of comparison (more tolerable). Thus prophecy, wisdom, and eschatology are combined to create a rather unique situation. The past informs the future which warns us, in the present, to prepare.

14 WOES ON GALILEE

Mt. 11:20–24	*Lk. 10:13–15*
(20) Then he began to upbraid the cities where most of his mighty works had been done, because they did not repent. (21) "Woe to you, Chorazin! woe to you, Bethsaida! for if the mighty works done in you had been done in Tyre and Sidon, they would have repented long ago in sackcloth and ashes. (22) But I tell you, it shall be more tolerable on the day of judgment for Tyre and Sidon than for you. (23) And you, Capernaum, will you be exalted to heaven? You shall be brought down to Hades. For if the mighty works done in you had been done in Sodom, it would have remained until this day. (24) But I tell you that it shall be more tolerable on the day of judgment for the land of Sodom than for you."	(13) "Woe to you, Chorazin! woe to you, Bethsaida! for if the mighty works done in you had been done in Tyre and Sidon, they would have repented long ago, sitting in sackcloth and ashes. (14) But it shall be more tolerable in the judgment for Tyre and Sidon than for you. (15) And you, Capernaum, will you be exalted to heaven? You shall be brought down to Hades."
	Lk. 10:12
	(12) "I tell you, it shall be more tolerable on that day for Sodom than for that town."
[See 11:24]	

Lk. 10:13 has been discussed above as a woe. In verses 14 and 15 the threat is expanded by a continued stress upon the way Tyre and Sidon have proven more acceptable than the Galilean cities. Verse 14

is a comparison statement sharing the same word used in the previous section (more tolerable). The eschatological dimension is close to apocalyptic with the judgment explicitly stated. But verse 14 must be considered a prophetic announcement, despite the wisdom tendency.

Verse 15 shows the same apocalyptic aspect with its reference to heaven and Hades and future-tense verbs. The comparison motif is present but expressed in a sarcastic rhetorical question and the expected opposite answer. This also is a prophetic saying which reveals the truth of the situation to be the opposite of that expected by the inhabitants of these cities.

The criticism of Galilee probably indicates a northern Palestinian environment for the Q community, but one in which success has been minimal. It is the non-Jew who has been more receptive to this message than the Jews of Jesus' homeland.

#15 WHOEVER HEARS YOU, HEARS ME

Mt. 10:40	*Lk. 10:16*
(40) "He who receives you receives me, and he who receives me receives him who sent me."	(16) "He who hears you hears me, and he who rejects you rejects me, and he who rejects me rejects him who sent me."

Redaction is once again quite evident but the form appears to have remained stable. The similarity to the *Satz heiligen Rechtes* (he who denies me will be denied by the father) is striking. Both forms use the conditional-relative sentence and both repeat the verb. However, the differences are just as striking. First the eschatological dimension is not present; the verbs are all in the present tense and the saying could be understood in a gnomic way. Second, there is a progression of three elements—the response to "you," the response to "me," and the implied response to the one who sent me. The result is an increased emphasis on the Q community and those who represent or speak for Jesus (and by analogy, the Father). Third, there is no judgmental activity of God stated here; the action of the person is not "returned" to him; rather it is simply that the implications of this action are more far-reaching than is apparent.

105

The phrase "the one who sent me" could be interpreted as a prophetic motif. But the sage is also one who feels sent by wisdom to communicate that understanding which comes from a clear grasp of the way the world works. The message is best understood as the simple drawing of conclusions based on the obvious fact that God is the one who has created the world and its resultant relationships. Thus prophetic and wisdom tendencies cannot be clearly distinguished from one another in this saying.

#16 THANKSGIVING AND BLESSEDNESS OF DISCIPLES

Mt. 11:25–27

(25) At that Jesus declared, "I thank thee, Father, Lord of Heaven and earth, that thou hast hidden these things from the wise and understanding and revealed them to babes; (26) yea, Father, for such was thy gracious will. (27) All things have been delivered to me by my Father; and no one knows the Son except the Father, and no one knows the Father except the Son and any one to whom the Son chooses to reveal him."

Mt. 13:16–17

(16) "But blessed are your eyes, for they see, and your ears, for they hear. (17) Truly, I say to you, many prophets and righteous men longed to see what you see, and did not see it, and to hear what you hear, and did not hear it."

Lk. 10:21–24

(21) In that same hour he rejoiced in the Holy Spirit and said, "I thank thee, Father, Lord of heaven and earth, that thou hast hidden these things from the wise and understanding and revealed them to babes; yea, Father, for such was thy gracious will. (22) All things have been delivered to me by my Father; and no one knows who the Son is except the Father, or who the Father is except the Son and any one to whom the Son chooses to reveal him."

(23) Then turning to the disciples he said privately, "Blessed are the eyes which see what you see! (24) For I tell you that many prophets and kings desired to see what you see, and did not see it, and to hear what you hear and did not hear it."

[See 10:23–24]

Lk. 10:21–22 contains one of the classic passages for those who appeal to a wisdom Christology in Q. It has been called a revealer speech and a thanksgiving. The Jesus of this speech speaks with a confidence and fluency which we have not seen previously reflected in the Q material. The basic theme is the revelation made known to the son which has not been made available to everyone—either because they are "too wise" or because they have not been favored by the Son, i.e., he does not reveal it to those who are unworthy.

A clear case is made here for the subordination of the son to the father, not at all like the wisdom introduction which is often condescending—"My son, listen to me . . ." The concepts of prophet and wise man come close together here in the idea of one being sent to do God's work. This combination, seen clearly in Sirach, seems to be a general assumption here. The father reveals understanding, but to *babes*, not to the traditional recipients of wisdom.

The beatitude has been discussed above. Luke places it immediately after the thanksgiving, Matthew elsewhere. But both evangelists seem to be implying that the point of the saying is its reference to the disciples as a continuation of the line of communication established by God through Jesus and now through the Q community. It is followed by the prophetic formula and a general wisdom statement which adds the emphasis of judgment.

#17 LORD'S PRAYER

Mt. 6:9–13	Lk. 11:1–4
(9) "Pray then like this:	(1) He was praying in a certain
Our Father who art in heaven,	place, and when he ceased, one of his
Hallowed be thy name.	disciples said to him, "Lord, teach us
(10) Thy kingdom come,	to pray, as John taught his disciples."
Thy will be done,	(2) And he said to them, "When you
On earth as it is in heaven.	pray, say:
(11) Give us this day our daily bread;	"Father, hallowed be thy name. Thy
(12) And forgive us our debts,	kingdom come. (3) Give us each day our
As we also have forgiven our debtors;	daily bread; (4) and forgive us our sins,
(13) And lead us not into temptation,	for we ourselves forgive every one who
But deliver us from evil."	is indebted to us; and lead us not
	into temptation."

Recent research has emphasized the eschatological implications in the prayer,[3] as well as the apparent earliness of Luke's version. Matthew's version shows all the signs of Jewish liturgical practice.

Whether the sentence "Thy kingdom come" is an authentic statement of Jesus or not, it certainly reflects the hope of the Q community for God's action in the future. P. Vielhauer and others have

---

3. Cf. Norman Perrin, *Rediscovering the Teaching of Jesus* (New York: Harper & Row, 1967), pp. 160–161 and *The Kingdom of God in the Teaching of Jesus* (Philadelphia: Westminster Press, 1963), pp. 192–198.

emphasized the lack of explicit connection between the expectation of the Kingdom and the hope for the appearance of the Son of Man both here and in other places in the synoptic tradition.[4]

The background for the petition in verse 3 ("Give us each day our daily bread") appears to be a wisdom-like assumption that God does assist his people by means of the regularity of his creation. The request is possibly for God to continue to uphold the created order which has supplied food up to this point. However, in relation to the previous statement, it may be a request for aid in these last days until the Kingdom finally arrives.

Verse 4a is more prophetic than wisdom-like: the act-consequence relationship is based on an understanding of God which is not founded on the ways of the world. The concept of forgiveness appears twice in Q, here and the statement about forgiveness being available for those who sin against the Son of Man but not for those who sin against the Holy Spirit (#25). The context for both these sayings is eschatological, the last days which are upon the community.

The final request (Lk. 11:4b) indicates the trials of the last days. It hints at a problem which confronts the community, but no specifics are mentioned. It may be a reflection of the pressure of persecution which is mentioned elsewhere.

#18 ENCOURAGEMENT TO PRAY

Mt. 7:7–11

(7) "Ask, and it will be given you; seek, and you will find; knock, and it will be opened to you. (8) For every one who asks receives, and he who seeks finds, and to him who knocks it will be opened. (9) Or what man of you, if his son asks him for a loaf, will give him a stone? (10) Or if he asks for a fish, will give him a serpent? (11) If you then, who are evil, know how to give good gifts to your children, how much more will your Father who is in

Lk. 11:9–13

(9) "And I tell you, Ask, and it will be given you; seek, and you will find; knock, and it will be opened to you. (10) For every one who asks receives, and he who seeks finds, and to him who knocks it will be opened. (11) What father among you, if his son asks for a fish, will instead of a fish give him a serpent; (12) or if he asks for an egg, will give him a scorpion? (13) If you then, who are evil, know how to give good gifts to your children, how much

4. P. Vielhauer, "Gottesreich und Menschensohn in der Verkündung Jesu," *Festschrift für Günther Dehn,* ed. W. Schneemelcher (Neukirchen: Verlag der Buchhandlung des Enziehungsveieins Neukirchen, 1957), pp. 51–79.

heaven give good things to those who
ask him!"

more will the heavenly Father give the
Holy Spirit to those who ask him!"

Verbal similarity in this entire section is quite complete, except within the examples where the specific images and grammatical structure change somewhat.

Verses 9 and 10 contain a typical wisdom-teaching technique of repetition—in the threefold use of similar phrases, in the tense of verbs, in the use of complements (ask-receive), and in the repetition of the threefold question with the opening imperative changing to a relative.

These gnomic statements take on eschatological significance when the future verbs are seen in the light of the coming judgment—and not as merely earthly consequences of persistent activity. In the second strophe, there are two present-tense verbs ("receives, finds"), but the final verb ("will be opened") is future. Verse 9 is an *admonition* and verse 10 is a *sentence*—an effective combination of forms which asserts the assurance of this community about its status in the future.

The grounds of this assurance are stated in the next verses. Although the details of the parable have been redacted somewhat, the basic idea and structure remains. The argument is the *kal wakomer*—the first of Hillel's rules—in which one argues from a major to a minor point or from a minor to a major. In this case the appeal is based on common experience (as is typical in wisdom arguments)—that of a father giving food to his son; he will do his best to fulfill the request. The use of a question and the negative way of stating the situation are also typical wisdom features. The conclusion, then, in Lk. 11:13, simply clairifies the point and makes explicit the argument from the lesser to the greater, from man to God. Here, then, is a prophetic emphasis within a wisdom argument. "How much more" implies that God's goodness is known to be more than that of the earthly father. The future verb ("will give") points to the time yet to come when God will act by giving to those who ask.

Thus, although the prophetic aspect is not so clear as it has been previously, we do have a combination of the three tendencies— eschatology, wisdom, and prophecy.

109

#19 BEELZEBUL CONTROVERSY

Mt. 12:22–30	*Mk. 3:22–27*	*Lk. 11:14–23*
(22) Then a blind and dumb demoniac was brought to him, and he healed him, so that the dumb man spoke and saw. (23) And all the people were amazed, and said, "Can this be the Son of David?" (24) But when the Pharisees heard it they said, "It is only by Beelzebul, the prince of demons, that this man casts out demons." (25) Knowing their thoughts, he said to them, "Every kingdom divided against itself is laid waste, and no city or house divided against itself will stand; (26) and if Satan casts out Satan, he is divided against himself; how then will his kingdom stand? (27) And if I cast out demons by Beelzebul, by whom do your sons cast them out? Therefore they shall be your judges. (28) But if it is by the Spirit of God that I cast out demons, then the kingdom of God has come upon you. (29) Or how can one enter a strong man's house and plunder his goods, unless he first binds the strong man? Then indeed he may plunder his house. (30) He who is not with me is against me, and he who does not gather with me scatters."	(22) And the scribes who came down from Jerusalem said, "He is possessed by Beelzebul, and by the prince of demons he casts out the demons." (23) And he called them to him, and said to them in parables, "How can Satan cast out Satan? (24) If a kingdom is divided against itself, that kingdom cannot stand. (25) And if a house is divided against itself, that house will not be able to stand. (26) And if Satan has risen up against himself and is divided, he cannot stand, but is coming to an end. (27) But no one can enter a strong man's house and plunder his goods, unless he first binds the strong man; then indeed he may plunder his house."	(14) Now he was casting out a demon that was dumb; when the demon had gone out, the dumb man spoke, and the people marveled. (15) But some of them said, "He casts out demons by Beelzebul, the prince of demons"; (16) while others, to test him, sought from him a sign from heaven. (17) But he, knowing their thoughts, said to them, "Every kingdom divided against itself is laid waste, and house falls upon house. (18) And if Satan also is divided against himself, how will his kingdom stand? For you say that I cast out demons by Beelzebul. (19) And if I cast out demons by Beelzebul, by whom do your sons cast them out? Therefore they shall be your judges. (20) But if it is by the finger of God that I cast out demons, then the kingdom of God has come upon you. (21) When a strong man, fully armed, guards his own palace, his goods are in peace; (22) but when one stronger than he assails him and overcomes him, he takes away his armor in which he trusted, and divides his spoil. (23) He who is not with me is against me, and he who does not gather with me scatters."

Mt. 9:32–34

(32) As they were going away, behold, a dumb

demoniac was brought to him. (33) And when the demon had been cast out, the dumb man spoke; and the crowds marveled, saying, "Never was anything like this seen in Israel." (34) But the Pharisees said, "He casts out demons by the prince of demons."

The Beelzebul controversy has been used to support a variety of opinions—about the significance of exorcism, about the relation of Mark to Matthew and Luke, and about the importance of the proclamation of the Kingdom of God. Lk. 11:19–20, which is not found in Mark, clearly fits the definition of Q used in this book.

The agreement between Matthew and Luke in Lk. 11:19–20 is exact—except for one word (Matthew: spirit, Luke: finger). Two of the three sentences are conditionals with the first question followed by "therefore." The issue is not whether Jesus can cast out demons, but rather, by whose authority he is exorcising. The Q material probably had some statement about a divided kingdom, but it is hard to isolate because of the similar material in Mark. The point in verses 19 and 20 is that the exorcism is a sign that the Kingdom of God is here or has arrived. The *Sitz* in the Q community was probably the conflict between the Q community and their Jewish opponents.

Note the number of times the conditional sentence appears. The structure is a very argumentative one—if such and such is the case, then. . . . Whether it is put in the form of a question or not, it implies that there are an order and relationship among things which are readily recognizable. Verse 19 is a fine example of how the conditional sentence contrasts with a more prophetic announcement or declaration. Once the rhetorical question has made its point by showing the logical relationship of the two items, the "therefore" clause draws the conclusion almost as if it were from God's point of view.

The section ends with a wisdom sentence using the conditional relative form. In this version the saying is pointedly exclusive, implying that the Q community is again attempting to clarify itself over against opponents.

#20 RETURN OF THE EVIL SPIRIT

Mt. 12:43–45	*Lk. 11:24–26*
(43) "When the unclean spirit has gone out of a man, he passes through waterless places seeking rest, but he finds none. (44) Then he says, 'I will return to my house from which I came.' And when he comes he finds it empty, swept, and put in order. (45) Then he goes and brings with him seven other spirits more evil than himself, and they enter and dwell there; and the last state of that man becomes worse than the first. So shall it be also with this evil generation."	(24) "When the unclean spirit has gone out of a man, he passes through waterless places seeking rest; and finding none he says, 'I will return to my house from which I came.' (25) And when he comes he finds it swept and put in order. (26) Then he goes and brings seven other spirits more evil than himself, and they enter and dwell there; and the last state of that man becomes worse than the first."

This parable is unusual in that it does not contain any reference to what some call the furniture of the first century. As a result, it could easily lend itself to allegorization. The explanation offered by the parable itself says that the last state is worse than the first, i.e., being infected by seven more-evil spirits (plus the one who returns) is worse than the original single possession, but we are given no hint about how to apply this warning.

Since both Matthew and Luke place it close to the Beelzebul controversy, it may have been used by Q to imply that exorcism in itself is no sure cure, that possession by a good spirit in the place of an evil one is necessary if the individual is to profit by the exorcism. Since both wisdom and prophecy are considered by Q to be the result of the spirit of God, this may be an indication that the Q community assumes that prophetic or wisdom activity is a natural function of all its members who continue to preach the message of Jesus.

Thus it might be that the "last state" of the person is to be understood eschatologically and that to prepare for Jesus' coming is to prepare for the judgment. Being prepared is thus to allow the spirit of God to come and to take the place of the evil spirit who has been evicted. Positive activity is required.

#21 SIGN OF JONAH

Mt. 12:38–42

(38) Then some of the scribes and Pharisees said to him, "Teacher, we wish to see a sign from you." (39) But he answered them, "An evil and adulterous generation seeks for a sign; but no sign shall be given to it except the sign of the prophet Jonah. (40) For as Jonah was three days and three nights in the belly of the whale, so will the Son of man be three days and three nights in the heart of the earth. (41) The men of Nineveh will arise at the judgment with this generation and condemn it; for they repented at the preaching of Jonah, and behold, something greater than Jonah is here. (42) The queen of the South will arise at the judgment with this generation and condemn it; for she came from the ends of the earth to hear the wisdom of Solomon, and behold, something greater than Solomon is here."

Mt. 16:1–4

(1) And the Pharisees and Sadducees came, and to test him they asked him to show them a sign from heaven. (2) He answered them, "When it is evening, you say, 'It will be fair weather; for the sky is red.' (3) And in the morning, 'It will be stormy today, for the sky is red and threatening.' You know how to interpret the appearance of the sky, but you cannot interpret the signs of the times. (4) An evil and adulterous generation seeks for a sign, but no sign shall be given to it except the sign of Jonah." So he left them and departed.

Mk. 8:11–12

(11) The Pharisees came and began to argue with him, seeking from him a sign from heaven, to test him. (12) And he sighed deeply in his spirit, and said, "Why does this generation seek a sign? Truly, I say to you, no sign shall be given to this generation."

Lk. 11:16

(16) while others, to test him, sought from him a sign from heaven.

Lk. 11:29–32

(29) When the crowds were increasing, he began to say, "This generation is an evil generation; it seeks a sign, but no sign shall be given to it except the sign of Jonah. (30) For as Jonah became a sign to the men of Nineveh, so will the Son of man be to this generation. (31) The queen of the South will arise at the judgment with the men of this generation and condemn them; for she came from the ends of the earth to hear the wisdom of Solomon, and behold, something greater than Solomon is here. (32) The men of Nineveh will arise at the judgment with this generation and condemn it; for they repented at the preaching of Jonah, and behold, something greater than Jonah is here."

I have analyzed the sign of Jonah in detail in a seperate mono-graph.[5] The conclusion presented there argues that the Q community explains Jesus' refusal to give a sign (a tradition they share with Mark) by adding the phrase "except the sign of Jonah" and also by appending the saying about Jonah and Solomon. The crucial verse is Lk. 11:30 (Mt. 12:40) which has the same structure in Matthew and Luke, even though each evangelist has his own content. The structure of this sentence, and three others in Q, is the eschatological correlative, which I argued was a sentence that directly reflects the Q theological stance. The inclusion of the title Son of Man in the eschatological correlative also demonstrates the importance of that title to the members of the community.[6]

The future verb in the second part of the correlative (Lk. 11:30b), as well as those in 11:31 and 11:32 referring to the "arising" of the queen of the South and the men of Nineveh, substantiates the escha-tological emphasis of the entire passage.

Prophetic characteristics are evident in the reference to the preach-ing of Jonah, the prophet, which led to the repentance of the Ninevites. The Lukan version of the correlative (11:30) is probably closer to the Q version than Matthew's reference to the sojourn in the heart of the earth.[7] Thus the Q community explains the sign of Jonah by a reference to the preaching of Jonah, and correlates it with the preaching of the Son of Man, the future judge, who has already completed his earthly activities, but whose work of proclamation is still being continued by the community.

The wisdom dimension of the saying is found first in the reference to the wisdom of Solomon. But Solomon's wisdom is less than that wisdom which is available now, in the words of the Son of Man. Secondly, the presence of a series of comparisons is typical of wisdom forms. The eschatological correlative combines the comparative tech-nique with the theme of eschatology. The repetitive character of the double-saying in 11:31–32, as well as the comparisons contained in

---

5. Richard A. Edwards, *The Sign of Jonah in the Theology of the Evangelists and Q,* Studies in Biblical Theology, #18 Second Series (London: SCM Press, 1971).
6. Richard A. Edwards, "The Eschatological Correlative as a *Gattung* in the New Testament," *ZNW* 60 (1969): 9–20.
7. This point and others are considered in detail in the monograph mentioned in note 5.

it, are significant. The phrase "a greater than" is also an important part of this saying.

The effect of the entire Q passage is striking. All of the elements that have been presented as typical of Q are present in this pericope —wisdom, prophecy, and eschatology. In addition, the positive attitude toward Gentiles within the context of this judgment is an important theme in Q.

#22 SOUND EYE

Mt. 6:22–23	*Lk. 11:34–36*
(22) "The eye is the lamp of the body. So, if your eye is sound, your whole body will be full of light; (23) but if your eye is not sound, your whole body will be full of darkness. If then the light in you is darkness, how great is the darkness!"	(34) "Your eye is the lamp of your body; when your eye is sound, your whole body is full of light; but when it is not sound, your body is full of darkness. (35) Therefore be careful lest the light in you be darkness. (36) If then your whole body is full of light, having no part dark, it will be wholly bright, as when a lamp with its rays gives you light."

The parable in 11:34 is a basic wisdom teaching which points to the obvious significance of a healthy eye and the disadvantages of a damaged eye. We have found a number of references to seeing and not seeing in Q and thus any attempt to explain this parable must be put into that context.

Lk. 11:34 assumes that the eye allows light to enter (and to enlighten the individual) if it is a "sound eye." If it is evil, however, it does not allow light to enter and the "body is darkened." But 11:35 complicates this analogy by referring to the possibility that the "light" in a person might be "darkness." The metaphoric intention is thus more obviously stated. Luke may be playing with word sounds: verse 34 ends with "full of darkness (*skoteinon*)" and verse 35 begins with "be careful (*skopei*)" or he may have found it already in Q.

#23 AGAINST THE PHARISEES

Mt. 23:4–36	*Mk. 7:1–9*	*Lk. 11:37–54*
(4) "They bind heavy burdens, hard to bear, and	(1) Now when the Pharisees gathered together	(37) While he was speaking, a Pharisee asked

lay them on men's shoulders; but they themselves will not move them with their finger. (5) They do all their deeds to be seen by men; for they make their phylacteries broad and their fringes long, (6) and they love the place of honor at feasts and the best seats in the synagogues, (7) and salutations in the market places, and being called rabbi by men. (8) But you are not to be called rabbi, for you have one teacher, and you are all brethren. (9) And call no man your father on earth, for you have one Father, who is in heaven. (10) Neither be called masters, for you have one master, the Christ. (11) He who is greatest among you shall be your servant; (12) whoever exalts himself will be humbled, and whoever humbles himself will be exalted.

(13) "But woe to you, scribes and Pharisees, hypocrites! because you shut the kingdom of heaven against men; for you neither enter yourselves, nor allow those who would enter to go in. (15) Woe to you, scribes and Pharisees, hypocrites! for you traverse sea and land to make a single proselyte, and when he becomes a proselyte, you make him twice as much a child of hell as yourselves.

(16) "Woe to you, blind guides, who say, 'If any one swears by the temple, it is nothing; but if any one

to him, with some of the scribes, who had come from Jerusalem, (2) they saw that some of his disciples ate with hands defiled, that is, unwashed. (3) (For the Pharisees, and all the Jews, do not eat unless they wash their hands, observing the tradition of the elders; (4) and when they come from the market place, they do not eat unless they purify themselves; and there are many other traditions which they observe, the washing of cups and pots and vessels of bronze.) (5) And the Pharisees and the scribes asked him, "Why do your disciples not live according to the tradition of the elders, but eat with hands defiled?" (6) And he said to them, "Well did Isaiah prophesy of you hypocrites, as it is written,

'This people honors me with their lips, but their heart is far from me;

(7)
in vain do they worship me, teaching as doctrines the precepts of men.'

(8) You leave the commandment of God, and hold fast the tradition of men."

(9) And he said to them, "You have a fine way of rejecting the commandment of God, in order to keep your tradition!"

him to dine with him; so he went in and sat at table. (38) The Pharisee was astonished to see that he did not first wash before dinner. (39) And the Lord said to him, "Now you Pharisees cleanse the outside of the cup and of the dish, but inside you are full of extortion and wickedness. (40) You fools! Did not he who made the outside make the inside also? (41) But give for alms those things which are within; and behold, everything is clean for you.

(42) "But woe to you Pharisees! for you tithe mint and rue and every herb, and neglect justice and the love of God; these you ought to have done, without neglecting the others. (43) Woe to you Pharisees! for you love the best seat in the synagogues and salutations in the market places. (44) Woe to you; for you are like graves which are not seen, and men walk over them without knowing it."

(45) One of the lawyers answered him, "Teacher, in saying this you reproach us also." (46) And he said, "Woe to you lawyers also! for you load men with burdens hard to bear, and you yourselves do not touch the burdens with one of your fingers. (47) Woe to you! for you build the tombs of the prophets whom your fathers killed. (48) So you are witnesses

swears by the gold of the temple, he is bound by his oath.' (17) You blind fools! For which is greater, the gold or the temple that has made the gold sacred? (18) And you say, 'If any one swears by the altar, it is nothing; but if any one swears by the gift that is on the altar, he is bound by his oath.' (19) You blind men! For which is greater, the gift or the altar that makes the gift sacred? (20) So he who swears by the altar, swears by it and by everything on it; (21) and he who swears by the temple, swears by it and by him who dwells in it; (22) and he who swears by heaven, swears by the throne of God and by him who sits upon it.

(23) "Woe to you, scribes and Pharisees, hypocrites! for you tithe mint and dill and cummin, and have neglected the weightier matters of the law, justice and mercy and faith; these you ought to have done, without neglecting the others. (24) You blind guides, straining out a gnat and swallowing a camel!

(25) "Woe to you, scribes and Pharisees, hypocrites! for you cleanse the outside of the cup and of the plate, but inside they are full of extortion and rapacity. (26) You blind Pharisee! first cleanse the inside of the cup and of the plate, that the outside also may be clean.

and consent to the deeds of your fathers; for they killed them, and you build their tombs. (49) Therefore also the Wisdom of God said, 'I will send them prophets and apostles, some of whom they will kill and persecute,' (50) that the blood of all the prophets, shed from the foundation of the world, may be required of this generation, (51) from the blood of Abel to the blood of Zechariah, who perished between the altar and the sanctuary. Yes, I tell you, it shall be required of this generation. (52) Woe to you lawyers! for you have taken away the key of knowledge; you did not enter yourselves, and you hindered those who were entering."

(53) As he went away from there the scribes and the Pharisees began to press him hard, and to provoke him to speak of many things, (54) lying in wait for him, to catch at something he might say.

(27) "Woe to you, scribes and Pharisees, hypocrites! for you are like whitewashed tombs, which outwardly appear beautiful, but within they are full of dead men's bones and all uncleanness. (28) So you also outwardly appear righteous to men, but within you are full of hypocrisy and iniquity.

(29) "Woe to you, scribes and Pharisees, hypocrites! for you build the tombs of the prophets and adorn the monuments of the righteous, (30) saying, 'If we had lived in the days of our fathers, we would not have taken part with them in shedding the blood of the prophets. (31) Thus you witness against yourselves, that you are sons of those who murdered the prophets. (32) Fill up, then, the measure of your fathers. (33) You serpents, you brood of vipers, how are you to escape being sentenced to hell? (34) Therefore I send you prophets and wise men and scribes, some of whom you will kill and crucify, and some you will scourge in your synagogues and persecute from town to town, (35) that upon you may come all the righteous blood shed on earth, from the blood of innocent Abel to the blood of Zechariah the son of Barachiah, whom you murdered between the sanctuary and the altar. (36) Truly, I say to you, all this will come upon this generation."

This is a long collection of basically prophetic material which piles one woe upon another to emphasize the condemnation of this generation. Both Matthew and Luke keep this material together, but their arrangements are quite different.

Lk. 11:39–44 contains prophetic woes discussed above. The emphasis in each saying concentrates on the hypocrisy of the Pharisees (and the Jewish establishment) because they use the law as a shield against real commitment.

In 11:47 an added indictment is stated—the establishment has destroyed the prophets yet they build tombs or memorials to their memory. 11:49–51 reaches a climax with the use of the phrase "the Wisdom of God said" in Luke and "I say" in Matthew. In a prophetic judgment this generation is criticized for causing the death of all the prophets. What the original Q introduction might have been, is impossible to tell. But we can recognize that Matthew and Luke ascribe to Jesus a place among those prophets. The Q context seems to demand that we recognize that the Q community understands itself as a part of the line of the persecuted prophets—a theme already noted elsewhere.

This is not a typical wisdom speech as we have defined it. It is rather a prophetic threat which recalls the activity of YHWH, or his wisdom, sending prophets in the past—and implying that the prophets of the present (Jesus and his followers, the Q community) are being treated in precisely the same way. Thus a prophetic announcement informs the present generation about the true character of the Q community—that it is God-sent. Nonetheless, there is an element of the wisdom style of argument when the experience of the past is used as a guide to the present. But it is the past in terms of an historical event and not the guaranteed continuity of earthly existence. Verse 51 ends with the prophetic introduction "I say to you" and a short, pointed reference to the judgment of this generation.

Lk. 11:52 is Luke's concluding woe found earlier in Matthew's arrangement. Not only will this generation be condemned for their misdeeds, they are also responsible for preventing many from becoming followers of Jesus and perhaps for the persecution of the Q community.

#24 FEARLESS CONFESSION

Mt. 10:26–33

(26) "So have no fear of them; for nothing is covered that will not be revealed, or hidden that will not be known. (27) What I tell you in the dark, utter in the light; and what you hear whispered, proclaim upon the housetops. (28) And do not fear those who kill the body but cannot kill the soul; rather fear him who can destroy both soul and body in hell. (29) Are not two sparrows sold for a penny? And not one of them will fall to the ground without your father's will. (30) But even the hairs of your head are all numbered. (31) Fear not, therefore; you are of more value than many sparrows. (32) So every one who acknowledges me before men, I also will acknowledge before my Father who is in heaven; (33) but whoever denies me before men, I also will deny before my Father who is in heaven."

Lk. 12:2–9

(2) "Nothing is covered up that will not be revealed, or hidden that will not be known. (3) Whatever you have said in the dark shall be heard in the light, and what you have whispered in private rooms shall be proclaimed upon the housetops.

(4) "I tell you, my friends, do not fear those who kill the body, and after that have no more that they can do. (5) But I will warn you whom to fear: fear him who, after he has killed, has power to cast into hell; yes, I tell you, fear him! (6) Are not five sparrows sold for two pennies? And not one of them is forgotten before God. (7) Why, even the hairs of your head are all numbered. Fear not; you are of more value than many sparrows.

(8) "And I tell you, every one who acknowledges me before men, the Son of man also will acknowledge before the angels of God; (9) but he who denies me before men will be denied before the angels of God."

Both Matthew and Luke agree about the order of this material within the pericope.

Lk. 12:2 and 3 are typical sentences which attempt to encapsulate the knowledge gained by experience. By themselves they add little to our understanding—until we read the admonition of 12:4 and 5— "do not fear those who kill the body" but fear those who would cast you into "Gehenna"! The point is that the persecution which the Q community now suffers because of their proclamation of the words of the risen Lord is of little significance in the light of the coming judgment.

There follows, then, in 12:6 and 7, two extended metaphors which share both wisdom and prophetic characteristics. The first part of 12:6 is a sentence phrased as a question followed in the second part by an announcement of YHWH's care or interest in a mere sparrow.

The first part of 12:7 is a prophetic announcement repeating the same theme—all your hairs are numbered. The climax then follows: do not fear, you are of more value than many sparrows.

The eschatological implications are clear. At the final judgment there are decisions made of utmost significance which must be kept in proper perspective. Although the persecution is real now, it is insignificant in the wider expanse of life.

Lk. 12:8 and 9, composed as conditional-relative statements, are Käsemann's *Satz heiligen Rechts*. The eschatological thrust of the entire section is now stated clearly—the final judgment before God is the ultimate criterion for action now. The tasks of the present are demanded by the final situation. One's response to Q and its message is a final decision, and to remain in the Q community, despite its troubles, is to be prepared for the end.

Wisdom influence is also present in the comparatives throughout the pericope and in the rhetorical question as well. The *Satz heiligen Rechts* follows a series of everyday, worldly comparisons, a typical characteristic of Q in combining wisdom and eschatology.

#25 SIN AGAINST THE HOLY SPIRIT

Mt. 12:31–32	Mk. 3:29–30	Lk. 12:10
(31) "Therefore I tell you, every sin and blasphemy will be forgiven men, but the blasphemy against the Spirit will not be forgiven. (32) And whoever says a word against the Son of man will be forgiven; but whoever speaks against the Holy Spirit will not be forgiven, either in this age or in the age to come."	(29) "but whoever blasphemes against the Holy Spirit never has forgiveness, but is guilty of an eternal sin"—(30) for they had said, "He has an unclean spirit."	(10) "And every one who speaks a word against the Son of man will be forgiven; but he who blasphemes against the Holy Spirit will not be forgiven."

This is a notoriously difficult passage in which we have a combination of the double and triple tradition. Matthew and Luke disagree on the context, Matthew, following Mark, keeps it with the Beelzebul controversy while Luke places it after the *Satz heiligen Rechts* noted above.

Formally, we have a conditional-relative sentence in which the verb of the apodosis is in the future tense. It is basically an eschatological statement even though it is close to the sentence wisdom form.

It is impossible to tell whether the Q community knew the double form of the saying. The only indication that they might is the future passive verb (in Matthew and Luke) against Mark's present tense, but this could be explained as assimilation from the same verb in the first part of the verse.

Why would the Q community wish to announce forgiveness to those who speak against the Son of Man? If this is a community in preparation for the end, it is possible that they desire to keep open the possibility of converts from among the Jews. The conditions for forgiveness are not stated, but the evidence so far seems to point to a requirement of joining the Q community, if one is to be properly prepared. Thus, they may be announcing the ultimate forgiveness of God for those who have become part of their community. The Son of Man is the judge at the end and his forgiveness is possible if some indication of change is evident—else, why the mission of the Q community? In other words, this is a message of hope to the Jews and others—it's not too late to join.

#26 ASSISTANCE OF THE HOLY SPIRIT

Mt. 10:19–20	*Mk. 13:11*	*Lk. 12:11–12*
(19) "When they deliver you up, do not be anxious how you are to speak or what you are to say; for what you are to say will be given to you in that hour; (20) for it is not you who speak, but the Spirit of your Father speaking through you."	(11)"And when they bring you to trial and deliver you up, do not be anxious beforehand what you are to say; but say whatever is given you in that hour, for it is not you who speak, but the Holy Spirit."	(11) "And when they bring you before the synagogues and the rulers and the authorities, do not be anxious how or what you are to answer or what you are to say; (12) for the Holy Spirit will teach you in that very hour what you ought to say."
		Lk. 21:14–15
		(14) "Settle it therefore in your minds, not to meditate beforehand how to answer; (15) for I will give

you a mouth and wisdom,
which none of your
adversaries will be able to
withstand or contradict."

The evidence for Q material is very slim but this pericope is often considered to be from Q because it shares a similar theme with the following pericope. Using the principles stated in an earlier chapter, this material is too fragmentary to uncover any theological or structural information.

#27 ANXIETY

Mt. 6:25–34

(25) "Therefore I tell you, do not be anxious about your life, what you shall eat or what you shall drink, nor about your body, what you shall put on. Is not life more than food, and the body more than clothing? (26) Look at the birds of the air: they neither sow nor reap nor gather into barns, and yet your heavenly Father feeds them. Are you not of more value than they? (27) And which of you by being anxious can add one cubit to his span of life? (28) And why are you anxious about clothing? Consider the lilies of the field, how they grow; they neither toil nor spin; (29) yet I tell you, even Solomon in all his glory was not arrayed like one of these. (30) But if God so clothes the grass of the field, which today is alive and tomorrow is thrown into the oven, will he not much more clothe you, O men of little faith? (31) Therefore do not be anxious, saying, 'What shall we eat?' or 'What shall we drink?' or 'What shall we wear?' (32) For the Gentiles seek all these things; and your heavenly Father knows that you need them all. (33) But seek first his kingdom and his righteousness, and all these things shall be yours as well.

(34) "Therefore do not be anxious about tomorrow, for tomorrow will be anxious for itself. Let the day's own trouble be sufficient for the day."

Lk. 12:22–32

(22) And he said to his disciples, "Therefore I tell you, do not be anxious about your life, what you shall eat, nor about your body, what you shall put on. (23) For life is more than food, and the body more than clothing. (24) Consider the ravens: they neither sow nor reap, they have neither storehouse nor barn, and yet God feeds them. Of how much more value are you than the birds! (25) And which of you by being anxious can add a cubit to his span of life? (26) If then you are not able to do as small a thing as that, why are you anxious about the rest? (27) Consider the lilies, how they grow; they neither toil nor spin; yet I tell you, even Solomon in all his glory was not arrayed like one of these. (28) But if God so clothes the grass which is alive in the field today and tomorrow is thrown into the oven, how much more will he clothe you, O men of little faith! (29) And do not seek what you are to eat and what you are to drink, nor be of anxious mind. (30) For all the nations of the world seek these things; and your Father knows that you need them. (31) Instead, seek his kingdom, and these things shall be yours as well.

(32) "Fear not, little flock, for it is your Father's good pleasure to give you the kingdom."

There is an amazing amount of agreement here, both in words and in order.

Lk. 12:22–23 is an admonition which is followed by an explanation. Although it opens with the prophetic introduction (Therefore I tell you), the saying itself is a wisdom admonition which concentrates on the fact that surface appearances are not the most significant.

Lk. 12:24–30 contains a series of sentences which appeal in a variety of ways to the evidence for the admonition. The evidence is primarily based on the appeal to the natural world and its balance and stability. If there is evidence for God's care (or wisdom) toward plants and animals, surely, it is assumed, God's care will be directed to man. The birds (raven in Luke) are cared for, and you are of more value than they (12:24). Man grows and develops by God's care and one cannot interfere with this, so why worry? (12:25). Even plant life (lilies) has a glory given by God which man cannot exceed; despite its short life, it is under God's care and you are more than plants (12:27–28). Lk. 12:29–30 changes the pattern somewhat by indicating that other humans (the nations) are anxious to no avail. God controls all and thus he knows your needs; he is the good father.

The section ends with another admonition (Lk. 12:31). To seek the Kingdom is not to be anxious; one should work for the Kingdom and be prepared for its coming by not being anxious about ephemeral things. God will take care of you in those areas where it *really* counts.

The eschatological dimension is not explicitly stated, except for the mention of the Kingdom at the conclusion. The mention of fire in Lk. 12:28 has apocalyptic overtones.

#28 TREASURES IN HEAVEN

Mt. 6:19–21

(19) "Do not lay up for yourselves treasures on earth, where moth and rust consume and where thieves break in and steal, (20) but lay up for yourselves treasures in heaven, where neither moth nor rust consumes and where thieves do not break in and steal. (21) For where your treasure is, there will your heart be also."

Lk. 12:33–34

(33) "Sell your possessions, and give alms; provide yourselves with purses that do not grow old, with a treasure in the heavens that does not fail, where no thief approaches and no moth destroys. (34) For where your treasure is, there will your heart be also."

Lk. 12:34 is a sentence. Lk. 12:33 shows extensive redaction on the part of Matthew or Luke; the remnants indicate that in Q there was some description of the possible kinds of treasure. The nonsubstantiality of earthly treasure is contrasted, in typical wisdom style, with the true heavenly treasure.

Lk. 12:34 is a forceful statement which simply verbalizes the earlier understanding. Matthew and Luke differ only in the personal pronouns (Matthew singular, Luke plural). With standard proverbial force, the comparative point is made: where—there.

#29 WATCHFULNESS AND FAITHFULNESS

Mt. 24:42–51

(42) "Watch therefore, for you do not know on what day your Lord is coming. (43) But know this, that if the householder had known in what part of the night the thief was coming, he would have watched and would not have let his house be broken into. (44) Therefore you also must be ready; for the Son of man is coming at an hour you do not expect.

(45) "Who then is the faithful and wise servant, whom his master has set over his household, to give them their food at the proper time? (46) Blessed is that servant whom his master when he comes will find so doing. (47) Truly, I say to you, he will set him over all his possessions. (48) But if that wicked servant says to himself, 'My master is delayed,' (49) and begins to beat his fellow servants, and eats and drinks with the drunken, (50) the master of that servant will come on a day when he does not expect him and at an hour he does not know, (51) and will punish him, and put him with the hypocrites; there men will weep and gnash their teeth."

Lk. 12:35–48

(35) "Let your loins be girded and your lamps burning, (36) and be like men who are waiting for their master to come home from the marriage feast, so that they may open to him at once when he comes and knocks. (37) Blessed are those servants whom the master finds awake when he comes; truly, I say to you, he will gird himself and have them sit at table, and he will come and serve them. (38) If he comes in the second watch, or in the third, and finds them so, blessed are those servants! (39) But know this, that if the householder had known at what hour the thief was coming, he would have been awake and would not have left his house to be broken into. (40) You also must be ready; for the Son of man is coming at an hour you do not expect."

(41) Peter said, "Lord, are you telling this parable for us or for all?" (42) And the Lord said, "Who then is the faithful and wise steward, whom his master will set over his household, to give them their portion of food at the proper time? (43) Blessed is that servant whom his master when he comes will find so doing. (44) Truly I tell you, he will set him over all his possessions. (45) But if that servant says

to himself, 'My master is delayed in coming,' and begins to beat the menservants and the maidservants, and to eat and drink and get drunk, (46) the master of that servant will come on a day when he does not expect him and at an hour he does not know, and will punish him, and put him with the unfaithful. (47) And that servant who knew his master's will, but did not make ready or act according to his will, shall receive a severe beating. (48) But he who did not know, and did what deserved a beating, shall receive a light beating. Every one to whom much is given, of him will much be required; and of him to whom men commit much they will demand the more."

The Q portion of this pericope shows a close similarity between Matthew and Luke in words and in order. The opening of the parable ("know this") could be a variant on the prophetic introduction. It occurs only once in Q but twice in the Markan tradition—from the apocalyptic discourse. It is possible that it is an apocalyptic counterpart to the prophetic "I say to you" and the wisdom introduction "Listen, my son."

The parable itself could be understood as apocalyptic or gnomic. But the admonition that follows (Lk. 12:40) makes the explicit assertion that the Son of Man is the one who comes unexpectedly, thus clearly stating the apocalyptic context. This particular verse could serve as a statement of *the* theme of the Q community—be ready for the Son of Man's coming.

Lk. 12:42 is a sentence put into a question form. The ideal follower of Jesus is like the good servant who can be given authority and responsibility without any question of his ability or timing. Preparation is not a separate activity but a way of life—to be prepared is to live constantly as a faithful, trusted servant. The beatitude in Lk. 12:43 (discussed above) reiterates the basic thought now in a beatitude form: be ready by never ceasing to do what is required. Following Jesus is a full-time commitment.

Lk. 12:44 uses the prophetic introduction to announce the activity of God which will take place; it also serves to summarize the previous material.

In Lk. 12:45–46 we have another statement of the same theme which may have been added because of a thematic connection but which creates some ambiguity about the purpose of 12:44. The parable illustrates the unfavorable servant's reaction and doesn't really continue the positive emphasis of the two previous verses. After the actions of the foolish or unprepared servant are detailed, the master's return is predicted and the certainty of the servant's punishment is confirmed. Thus the apocalyptic emphasis is reasserted again at the end of the collection implying that the Q community feels that it lives in the interim.

#30 DIVISIONS IN HOUSEHOLDS

Mt. 10:34–36	Lk. 12:49–53
(34) "Do not think that I have come to bring peace on earth; I have not come to bring peace, but a sword. (35) For I have come to set a man against his father, and a daughter against her mother, and a daughter-in-law against her mother-in-law; (36) and a man's foes will be those of his own household."	(49) "I came to cast fire upon the earth; and would that it were already kindled! (50) I have a baptism to be baptized with; and how I am constrained until it is accomplished! (51) Do you think that I have come to give peace on earth? No, I tell you, but rather division; (52) for henceforth in one house there will be five divided, three against two and two against three; (53) they will be divided, father against son and son against father, mother against daughter and daughter against her mother, mother-in-law against daughter-in-law and daughter-in-law against her mother-in-law."

The agreement in this passage is minimal and thus forms cannot be reconstructed. But the slight verbal agreement is enhanced by the similarity of subject matter. In Lk. 12:51 "peace on the earth" is not the object of Jesus' appearance but rather he comes to bring unrest or division. Even though Lk. 12:53 merely contains similar nouns denoting family members, the intent is the same for Matthew and Luke, viz., the normal family relationships will not be important.

In the light of other references to persecution and the trouble to be expected among those who belong to this community, this material is thematically consistent with the rest of Q. Participating in the Q community demands a rejection of normal family relationships. The apocalyptic dimension is present in the reversal of normal conditions. Since there is little indication of any wisdom style, the emphasis is prophetic, i.e., an announcement of that which will be.

#31 SIGNS OF THE TIMES

Mt. 16:2–3
(2) He answered them, "When it is evening, you say, 'It will be fair weather; for the sky is red.' (3) And in the morning, 'It will be stormy today, for the sky is red and threatening.' You know how to interpret the appearance of the sky, but you cannot interpret the signs of the times."

Lk. 12:54–56
(54) He also said to the multitudes, "When you see a cloud rising in the west, you say at once, 'A shower is coming'; and so it happens. (55) And when you see the south wind blowing, you say, 'There will be scorching heat'; and it happens. (56) You hyprocrites! You know how to interpret the appearance of earth and sky; but why do you not know how to interpret the present time?"

Verbal agreement is minimal and not extensive enough to indicate forms. Nevertheless, the subject matter is quite similar—the prediction of weather on the evidence of currrent conditions. This so-called scientific method is actually good wisdom procedure: use your practical experience and the current data to come to an understanding of the way things usually work.

The contrast stated is between the "fact of the heavens," the available evidence which is used to predict the future conditions, and the present time which "they" cannot interpret or understand. How we are to understand the word "the times (the present time)" is hard to say. The context seems to imply a reference to the authority of the Son of Man (in his activity as judge), the gift of the spirit, or the meaning of his persecution (and that of the Q community).

#32 AGREEMENT WITH ACCUSER

Mt. 5:25–26
(25) "Make friends quickly with your accuser, while you are going with him to court, lest your accuser hand you over to the judge, and the judge to the guard, and you be put in prison;

Lk. 12:57–59
(57) "And why do you not judge for yourselves what is right? (58) As you go with your accuser before the magistrate, make an effort to settle with him on the way, lest he drag

(26) truly, I say to you, you will never get out till you have paid the last penny."	you to the judge, and the judge hand you over to the officer, and the officer put you in prison. (59) I tell you, you will never get out till you have paid the very last copper."

Lk. 12:58–59 combines a wisdom admonition with a prophetic pronouncement. Relying on conventional experience, you are advised to settle the matter "on the way" to the judge, lest you be incarcerated and thus unable to do a thing. Formally, 12:59 is a sentence but with the prophetic introduction it becomes an announcement which is categorically asserted as a threat. Thus once again, the prophetic and wisdom themes come together.

A community under persecution or distress would find this kind of advice quite helpful. If the end is near, it is best to avoid any unnecessary restraints and work to one's limit.

#33 MUSTARD SEED

Mt. 13:31–32	Mk. 4:30–32	Lk. 13:18–19
(31) Another parable he put before them, saying, "The kingdom of heaven is like a grain of mustard seed which a man took and sowed in his field; (32) it is the smallest of all seeds, but when it has grown it is the greatest of shrubs and becomes a tree, so that the birds of the air come and make nests in its branches."	(30) And he said, "With what can we compare the kingdom of God, or what parable shall we use for it? (31) It is like a grain of mustard seed, which, when sown upon the ground, is the smallest of all the seeds on earth; (32) yet when it is sown it grows up and becomes the greatest of all shrubs, and puts forth large branches, so that the birds of the air can make nests in its shade."	(18) He said therefore, "What is the kingdom of God like? And to what shall I compare it? (19) It is like a grain of mustard seed which a man took and sowed in his garden; and it grew and became a tree, and the birds of the air made nests in its branches."

It has been argued that the parable of the mustard seed was found in both Mark and Q. Despite Luke's apparently extensive deletions, there are some precise agreements with Matthew which could indicate a separate version.

It is impossible to isolate any significant Q formal structures. As a parable, it is related to a wisdom approach to instruction.

129

#34 LEAVEN

Mt. 13:33

(33) He told them another parable.
"The kingdom of heaven is like leaven
which a woman took and hid in three
measures of meal, till it was
all leavened."

Lk. 13:20–21

(20) And again he said, "To what
shall I compare the kingdom of God?
(21) It is like leaven which a woman
took and hid in three measures of
meal, till it was all leavened."

Both Matthew and Luke place this parable about leaven immediately after the mustard seed. Although introductions differ, the short comparison itself is almost exactly the same. Both introductions show evidence of a connection between this parable and the previous one: Luke says, "And *again* he said" while Matthew says, "He told them *another* parable."

The wisdom basis for this comparison is obvious. It is part of common knowledge that leaven must be "hidden" in flour in order to do its work. The emphasis seems to be upon the power of the leaven to affect the entire batch of dough. However, the verb "hid" (in Luke) and its intensification by Matthew is nowhere else used in conjunction with leaven and may be part of the emphasis of the comparison; that which is present is not always obvious.

The structure of the comparison implies a time lag: (1) the stating of the two items being compared, (2) a relative pronoun followed by the action, and (3) "until" introducing the result of the action.

Thus we have a wisdom parable with a bare minimum of information and with no conclusion or admonition.

#35 EXCLUSION FROM THE KINGDOM

Mt. 7:13–14

(13) "Enter by the narrow gate; for
the gate is wide and the way is easy,
that leads to destruction, and those who
enter by it are many. (14) For the gate
is narrow and the way is hard, that
leads to life, and those who find it are
few."

Mt. 7:22–23

(22) "On that day many will say to
me, 'Lord, Lord, did we not prophesy
in your name, and cast out demons
in your name, and do many mighty

Lk. 13:22–30

(22) He went on his way through
towns and villages, teaching, and
journeying toward Jerusalem. (23) And
some one said to him, "Lord, will those
who are saved be few? And he said to
them, (24) "Strive to enter by the narrow
door; for many, I tell you, will seek
to enter and will not be able. (25) When
once the householder has risen up and
shut the door, you will begin to stand
outside and to knock at the door saying,
'Lord, open to us.' He will answer you,
'I do not know where you come from.'

works in your name?' (23) And then will I declare to them, 'I never knew you; depart from me, you evildoers.' "

Mt. 8:11–12
(11) "I tell you, many will come from east and west and sit at table with Abraham, Isaac, and Jacob in the kingdom of heaven, (12) while the sons of the kingdom will be thrown into the outer darkness; there men will weep and gnash their teeth."

Mt. 19:30
(30) "But many that are first will be last, and the last first."

(26) Then you will begin to say, 'We ate and drank in your presence, and you taught in our streets.' (27) But he will say, 'I tell you, I do not know where you come from; depart from me, all you workers of iniquity!' (28) There you will weep and gnash your teeth, when you see Abraham and Isaac and Jacob and all the prophets in the kingdom of God and you yourselves thrust out. (29) And men will come from east and west, and from north and south, and sit at table in the kingdom of God. (30) And behold, some are last who will be first, and some are first who will be last."

This passage exhibits complex and fragmentary interrelation between Matthew and Luke. Little can be said about the form as such. Prophetic, apocalyptic, and wisdom characteristics are all evident with Matthew and Luke apparently using the material in quite varied ways.

In Lk. 13:24 the comparison is between a wide and narrow gate. Luke's introduction creates an apophthegm which relates the saying to a question about how one can be saved and to the general theme of "journeying while teaching." Matthew has simply included a longer more complex comparison in a collection of sayings in the Sermon on the Mount (7:13–14).

The Q material is too fragmentary to allow a reconstruction of forms. But the material we do have is an admonition to choose the narrow or more difficult way. "Many" describes those who are rejected and who are either unable to achieve (Luke) or who merely choose the wider and easier way. Matthew's more symmetrical and repetitious form could be the older.

Although the subject of Lk. 13:25 and Mt. 7:22 is similar, the verbal similarity is limited to the address "Lord." Both evangelists emphasize the rejection of pseudo-believers and in 13:27 (Mt. 7:23) they are described as those who have not *done* things required. Both evangelists describe them as those whose works are defective. Thus

131

we have the remains of a prophetic rejection with its emphasis on the significance of Jesus: "depart *from me*."

Luke places the Q phrase "there will be weeping and gnashing of teeth" at the beginning of the next section, Matthew at the end. This arrangement could be explained in two ways: Luke, "you" see Abraham and Isaac and Jacob and all the prophets *in* the Kingdom of God and yourselves thrust out; Matthew, using the phrase as a conclusion, says it is because "they" are cast out while the many who are chosen are inside eating with the patriarchs (no prophets mentioned).

The final result is a prophetic parable with a warning almost functioning as a sentence. It comes about as close to an apocalyptic passage as we can find in Q.

#36 LAMENT OVER JERUSALEM

Mt. 23:37–39	*Lk. 13:34–35*
(37) "O Jerusalem, Jerusalem, killing the prophets and stoning those who are sent to you! How often would I have gathered your children together as a hen gathers her brood under her wings, and you would not! (38) Behold, your house is forsaken and desolate. (39) For I tell you, you will not see me again, until I say, 'Blessed is he who comes in the name of the Lord.' "	(35) "O Jerusalem, Jerusalem, killing the prophets and stoning those who are sent to you. How often would I have gathered your children together as a hen gathers her brood under her wings, and you would not! (35) Behold, your house is forsaken. And I tell you, you will not see me until you say, 'Blessed be he who comes in the name of the Lord.' "

This well-known saying is almost identical in Matthew and Luke. The variations are minor and stylistic except for "again" in Mt. 23:39.

These two verses (three in Matthew) contain a wide variety of forms. Although the term "lament" is applicable, the first part is a wisdom speech with a typical wisdom analogy—the hen who protects her chicks. Although a warning is implied, the perversity of the city is merely recorded. The result of this perversity is stated in a prophetic announcement which is a quote from Jer. 22:5. Finally, with a prophetic introduction ("I tell you") the section is concluded with an admonition which requires the believer to recognize Jesus as the one with authority by pronouncing a beatitude—a quote from Ps. 118:26.

The thrust of the entire saying is to castigate those Jews who do not recognize Jesus as the one sent by YHWH. References to prophets are frequent in Q and the prophets are particularly important in Q's definition of their role as Jesus' followers, indeed, as persecuted followers. This emphasis in underlined by the quotation from Jeremiah and the prophetic introduction to the concluding admonition. A prophetic consciousness is combined with the recognition that Jesus will return and that recognition of his authority is the only way to survive the judgment.

The Q community has therefore used both wisdom and prophetic forms and images to present its "case" against the non-Christian Jew. Jerusalem has rejected YHWH's help by persecuting the prophets and rejecting his protection; thus, they are doomed. The solution is to accept YHWH's help, as it is available in Jesus, and from those who speak his word (those who come in the name of the Lord).

#37 GREAT SUPPER

Mt. 22:1–14

(1) And again Jesus spoke to them in parables, saying, (2) "The kingdom of heaven may be compared to a king who gave a marriage feast for his son, (3) and sent his servants to call those who were invited to the marriage feast; but they would not come. (4) Again he sent other servants, saying, 'Tell those who are invited, Behold, I have made ready my dinner, my oxen and my fat calves are killed, and everything is ready; come to the marriage feast.' (5) But they made light of it and went off, one to his farm, another to his business, (6) while the rest seized his servants, treated them shamefully, and killed them. (7) The king was angry, and he sent his troops and destroyed those murderers and burned their city. (8) Then he said to his servants, 'The wedding is ready, but

Lk. 14:15–24

(15) When one of those who sat at table with him heard this, he said to him, "Blessed is he who shall eat bread in the kingdom of God!" (16) But he said to him, "A man once gave a great banquet, and invited many; (17) and at the time for the banquet he sent his servant to say to those who had been invited, 'Come; for all is now ready.' (18) But they all alike began to make excuses. The first said to him, 'I have bought a field, and I must go out and see it; I pray you, have me excused.' (19) And another said, 'I have bought five yoke of oxen, and I go to examine them; I pray you, have me excused.' (20) And another said, 'I have married a wife, and therefore I cannot come.' (21) So the servant came and reported this to his master. Then the householder in

133

those invited were not worthy. (9) Go therefore to the thoroughfares, and invite to the marriage feast as many as you find.' (10) And those servants went out into the streets and gathered all whom they found, both bad and good; so the wedding hall was filled with guests.

(11) "But when the king came in to look at the guests, he saw there a man who had no wedding garment; (12) and he said to him, 'Friend, how did you get in here without a wedding garment?' And he was speechless. (13) Then the king said to the attendants, 'Bind him hand and foot, and cast him into the outer darkness; there men will weep and gnash their teeth.' (14) For many are called, but few are chosen."

anger said to his servant, 'Go out quickly to the streets and lanes of the city, and bring in the poor and maimed and blind and lame.' (22) And the servant said, 'Sir, what you commanded has been done, and still there is room.' (23) And the master said to the servant, 'Go out to the highways and hedges, and compel people to come in, that my house may be filled. (24) For I tell you, none of those men who were invited shall taste my banquet.' "

The redactional activity of Matthew and Luke is so widely recognized that we can assume it here. The verbal agreement is very minimal and mostly in the opening sentences of the parable itself. What it may have been like in Q is impossible to say; that it was there, seems quite evident. A parable about a feast with invited guests who are summoned isn't much to go on.

No language structures of Q are evident in the fragments. We can only note that the parable form itself is present with its wisdom-teaching possibilities.

#38 CONDITIONS OF DISCIPLESHIP

Mt. 10:37–38

(37) "He who loves father or mother more than me is not worthy of me; and he who loves son or daughter more than me is not worthy of me; (38) and he who does not take his cross and follow me is not worthy of me."

Lk. 14:25–33

(25) Now great multitudes accompanied him; and he turned and said to them, (26) "If any one come to me and does not hate his own father and mother and wife and children and brothers and sisters, yes, and even his own life, he cannot be my disciple. (27) Whoever does not bear his own cross and come after me, cannot be my disciple. (28) For which of you, desiring to build a tower, does not first sit down and count the cost, whether he has enough to complete it? (29)

Otherwise, when he has laid a foundation, and is not able to finish, all who see it begin to mock him, (30) saying, 'This man began to build, and was not able to finish.' (31) Or what king, going to encounter another king in war, will not sit down first and take counsel whether he is able with ten thousand to meet him who comes against him with twenty thousand? (32) And if not, while the other is yet a great way off, he sends an embassy and asks terms of peace. (33) So therefore, whoever of you does not renounce all that he has cannot be my disciple."

This is the only place in Q where the cross is mentioned or where there is even a hint at the significance of the death of Jesus. We have seen plenty of references to persecution and especially the death of the prophets. However, even here, the point seems to be the need to accept responsibilities other than normal familial obligations. Similar material in Lk. 12:53 (Mt. 10:35) in the saying about *not* bringing peace and in Lk. 9:59 (Mt. 8:21) about not allowing a son to bury his father may indicate a subtheme in Q about the tendency of family ties to hinder those who are trying to meet the obligations of the community. The word "father" is also used to refer to the previous generations usually in a derogatory way, and may also indicate a related theme.

The major point to be noted is the emphasis on the need to follow, i.e., to be a disciple, and that discipleship in this community demands the utmost.

#39 PARABLE OF SALT

Mt. 5:13

(13) "You are the salt of the earth; but if salt has lost its taste, how shall its saltness be restored? It is no longer good for anything except to be thrown out and trodden under foot by men."

Mk. 9:49–50

(49) "For every one will be salted with fire. (50) Salt is good; but if the salt has lost its saltness, how will you season it? Have salt in yourselves, and be at peace with one another."

Lk. 14:34–35

(34) "Salt is good; but if salt has lost its taste, how shall its saltness be restored? (35) It is fit neither for the land nor for the dunghill; men throw it away. He who has ears to hear, let him hear."

135

There is enough precise agreement between Matthew and Luke against Mark, that we can suggest the existence of a Q comparison about salt. Matthew and Luke agree in using "has lost its taste" against Mark's "has lost its saltness." This same Q word is used by Paul as the reverse of wisdom (1 Cor. 1:20 and Rom. 1:22) (cf. Jer. 10:14 and Sir. 23:14).

In addition, Matthew and Luke agree about the fate of salt-less salt—it is cast out—an image of judgment.

Structurally there is nothing complete enough to be useful. But a comparison about the judgment against "foolish" salt is in character with the wisdom approach of seeking analogies and is consistent in judging on the basis of performance.

#40 LOST SHEEP

Mt. 18:12–14

(12) "What do you think? If a man has a hundred sheep, and one of them has gone astray, does he not leave the ninety-nine on the hills and go in search of the one that went astray? (13) And if he finds it, truly, I say to you, he rejoices over it more than over the ninety-nine that never went astray. (14) So it is not the will of my father who is in heaven that one of these little ones should perish."

Lk. 15:1–7

(1) Now the tax collectors and sinners were all drawing near to hear him. (2) And the Pharisees and the scribes murmured, saying, "This man receives sinners and eats with them."

(3) So he told them this parable: (4) "What man of you, having a hundred sheep, if he has lost one of them, does not leave the ninety-nine in the wilderness, and go after the one which is lost, until he finds it? (5) And when he has found it, he lays it on his shoulders, rejoicing. (6) And when he comes home, he calls together his friends and his neighbors, saying to them, 'Rejoice with me, for I have found my sheep which was lost.' (7) Even so, I tell you, there will be more joy in heaven over one sinner who repents than over ninety-nine righteous persons who need no repentance."

Redactional activity has been too extensive here also to allow any analysis of structure. The varying placement of the prophetic introduction may indicate editorial adjustment by Matthew and Luke.

The parable has the usual wisdom approach of stating the commonplace and drawing a conclusion which is applicable to the author's situation. Both Matthew and Luke use "so" (the same word in Greek, *houtos*) followed by a reference to "heaven" in the conclusion. We have seen this before in the second part of the eschatological correlative. Thus it could be argued that the parable itself is similar to an extended opening of an eschatological correlative ("as it was . . .") with the emphasis placed on the commonplace (and not on the historical, OT past). It means that the wisdom influence has caused a "shift" toward the universal as the community elaborates its eschatological understanding.

Wisdom, prophecy, and eschatology are once again combined.

#41 TWO MASTERS

Mt. 6:24	*Lk. 16:13*
(24) "No one can serve two masters; for either he will hate the one and love the other, or he will be devoted to the one and depise the other. You cannot serve God and mammon."	(13) "No servant can serve two masters; for either he will hate the one and love the other, or he will be devoted to the one and despise the other. You cannot serve God and mammon."

Verbal similarity is exact except for the word "servant" which Luke adds at the beginning.

Structurally this is an expanded sentence which states a truth in its most limited terms, then amplifies the statement, and finally concludes by precisely defining the two potential masters—God and Mammon. A worldly situation is given precise religious significance.

This is similar to the wisdom theme of the "two ways" which we find in the *Didache,* among other places.

#42 CONCERNING THE LAW

Mt. 11:12–13	*Lk. 16:16–17*
(12) "From the days of John the Baptist until now the kingdom of heaven has suffered violence, and men of violence take it by force. (13) For all the prophets and the law prophesied until John."	(16) "The law and the prophets were until John; since then the good news of the kingdom of God is preached, and every one enters it violently. (17) But it is easier for heaven and earth to pass away, than for one dot of the law to become void.
Mt. 5:18	
(18) "For truly, I say to you, till	

heaven and earth pass away, not an
iota, not a dot, will pass from the law
until all is accomplished."

Matthew and Luke do not agree in placing these two sayings together and redactional activity is evident. The result is some agreement in language, but no comparable formal structure.

The emphasis in Lk. 16:16 is upon John and his role in the coming of the Kingdom. "Violently (violence)" seems to imply persecution—a theme we have seen often enough in Q especially in relation to the prophets.

The thrust of the statement is prophetic.

Lk. 16:17 is also fragmentary and exhibits two different methods of expression. Mk. 13:31 (par. Mt. 24:35 and Lk. 21:33) from the apocalyptic speech indicates a common theme in the tradition. Although there is some prophetic thrust to the statement, the comparative approach and the reference to the "natural world" indicates a wisdom background. The eternality of the law is assumed and provides a basis for comparison.

#43 WARNING AGAINST OFFENSES

Mt. 18:6–7	*Mk. 9:42*	*Lk. 17:1–3a*
(6) "But whoever causes one of these little ones who believe in me to sin, it would be better for him to have a great millstone fastened round his neck and to be drowned in the depth of the sea. (7) "Woe to the world for temptations to sin! For it is necessary that temptations come, but woe to the man by whom the temptation comes!"	(42) "Whoever causes one of these little ones who believe in me to sin, it would be better for him if a great millstone were hung round his neck and he were thrown into the sea."	(1) And he said to his disciples, "Temptations to sin are sure to come; but woe to him by whom they come! (2) It would be better for him if a millstone were hung round his neck and he were cast into the sea, than that he should cause one of these little ones to sin. (3a) Take heed to yourselves; . . ."

This is another example of Q additions attached to material which is also in Mark. Matthew places it after Mark's passage, Luke before; probably attracted to each other by the catchword—"to sin" (*skandalon*).

The woe is incorporated into the saying; it cannot stand on its own. Matthew may be more original—with a double woe and with the dative case following the word "woe" in both places (and not at all in Luke's single woe).

#44 ON FORGIVENESS

Mt. 18:15

(15) "If your brother sins against you, go and tell him his fault, between him and you alone. If he listens to you, you have gained your brother."

Mt. 18:21–22

(21) Then Peter came up and said to him, "Lord, how often shall my brother sin against me, and I forgive him? As many as seven times?" (22) Jesus said to him, "I do not say to you seven times, but seventy times seven."

Lk. 17:3b–4

(3b) ". . . if your brother sins, rebuke him, and if he repents, forgive him; (4) and if he sins against you seven times in the day, and turns to you seven times, and says, 'I repent,' you must forgive him."

The agreement in 17:3b is the first part of a conditional relative form; the second parts differ in vocabulary although they agree in intent. In 17:4 no form is available; agreement is only in the numbers. The context is quite different.

#45 ON FAITH

Mt. 17:19–20

(19) Then the disciples came to Jesus privately and said, "Why could we not cast it out?" (20) He said to them, "Because of your little faith. For truly, I say to you, if you have faith as a grain of mustard seed, you will say to this mountain, 'Move hence to yonder place,' and it will move; and nothing will be impossible to you."

Mk. 9:28–29

(28) And when he had entered the house, his disciples asked him privately, "Why could we not cast it out?" (29) And he said to them, "This kind cannot be driven out by anything but prayer."

Lk. 17:5–6

(5) The apostles said to the Lord, "Increase our faith!" (6) And the Lord said, "If you had faith as a grain of mustard seed, you could say to this sycamine tree, 'Be rooted up, and be planted in the sea,' and it would obey you."

This is another conditional relative inserted into a section of Mark. It is used in the context of the disciples' question about their own inabilities to perform an exorcism. (Luke reports it as a simple request for faith.) The similar Markan context implies that the Q context was also that of the working of wonders—probably exorcisms. Neither Matthew nor Luke mention the word "prayer" which is the main point of Mark's answer.

The first part of the condition is almost identical in Matthew and Luke but the second part is significantly different. Both begin the second part with "say" but differ from that point on. Nevertheless, the images are similar, both referring to the displacement of apparently immovable objects and both ending with a statement about the confidence which is necessary (Matthew: "and nothing will be impossible for you"; Luke: "and it would obey you"). Thus we have a similar structure as a background for each evangelist's redaction: a conditional sentence with the second part describing very graphically what can be done, followed by a simple statement of the required conclusion.

The word "faith" appears four times in Q.

Luke	Matthew	
7:9	8:10	the centurion's faith
12:42	24:45	faithful servant (parable of the wise servant)
17:6	17:20	faith as a mustard seed
19:17	25:21	"because you have been faithful" (parable of pounds)

Each occurrence is in a context where faith or faithfulness is acted out in some specific way—by word or deed. Thus the context for the use of the word faith is that of the wisdom-prophetic approach to action—by their fruits you shall know them.

#46 DAY OF THE SON OF MAN

Mt. 24:23	Mk. 13:19–23	Lk. 17:22–37
(23) "Then if any one says to you, 'Lo, here is the Christ!' or 'There he is!' do not believe it." Mt. 24:26–27 (26) "So, if they say to	(19) "For in those days there will be such tribulation as has not been from the beginning of the creation which God created until now, and never will be. (20) And if the Lord had	(22) And he said to the disciples, "The days are coming when you will desire to see one of the days of the Son of man, and you will not see it. (23) And they will say to you, 'Lo,

you, 'Lo, he is in the wilderness,' do not go out; if they say, 'Lo, he is in the inner rooms,' do not believe it. (27) For as the lightning comes from the east and shines as far as the west, so will be the coming of the Son of man."

Mt. 24:37–39

(37) "As were the days of Noah, so will be the coming of the Son of man. (38) For as in those days before the flood they were eating and drinking, marrying and giving in marriage, until the day when Noah entered the ark, (39) and they did not know until the flood came and swept them all away, so will be the coming of the Son of man."

Mt. 24:17–18

(17) Let him who is on the housetop not go down to take what is in his house; (18) and let him who is in the field not turn back to take his mantle.

Mt. 10:39

(39) "He who finds his life will lose it, and he who loses his life for my sake will find it."

Mt. 24:40–41

(40) "Then two men will be in the field; one is taken and one is left. (41) Two women will be grinding at the mill; one is taken and one is left."

not shortened the days, no human being would be saved; but for the sake of the elect, whom he chose, he shortened the days. (21) And then if any one says to you, 'Look, here is the Christ!' or 'Look, there he is!' do not believe it. (22) False Christs and false prophets will arise and show signs and wonders, to lead astray, if possible, the elect. (23) But take heed; I have told you all things beforehand."

Mk. 13:14–16

(14) "But when you see the desolating sacrilege set up where it ought not to be (let the reader understand), then let those who are in Judea flee to the mountains; (15) let him who is on the housetop not go down, nor enter his house, to take anything away; (16) and let him who is in the field not turn back to take his mantle."

there!' or Lo, here!' Do not go, do not follow them. (24) For as the lightning flashes and lights up the sky from one side to the other, so will the Son of man be in his day. (25) But first he must suffer many things and be rejected by this generation. (26) As it was in the days of Noah so will it be in the days of the Son of man. (27) They ate, they drank, they married, they were given in marriage, until the day when Noah entered the ark, and the flood came and destroyed them all. (28) Likewise as it was in the days of Lot—they ate, they planted, they built, (29) but on the day when Lot went out from Sodom fire and brimstone rained from heaven and destroyed them all—(30) so will it be on the day when the Son of man is revealed. (31) On that day, let him who is on the housetop, with his goods in the house, not come down to take them away; and likewise let him who is in the field not turn back. (32) Remember Lot's wife. (33) Whoever seeks to gain his life will lose it; but whoever loses his life will preserve it. (34) I tell you, in that night there will be two men in one bed; one will be taken and the other left. (35) There will be two women grinding together; one will be taken and the other left."

Mt. 24:28

(28) "Wherever the body is, there the eagles will be gathered together."

(37) And they said to him, "Where, Lord?" He said to them, "Where the body is, there the eagles will be gathered together."

This section contains three of the four eschatological correlatives.[8] In fact, the future tense is present in every segment of this section. The conditional relative in Lk. 17:33 could be understood as a simple gnomic aphorism if it were viewed in isolation. In this context, however, it verges on an apocalyptic statement. 17:35 is clearly apocalyptic thought, emphasized by the opening "there will be." 17:37 is a sentence with a future verb in the conclusion.

The interaction of wisdom and prophecy with eschatology is quite far-reaching. The appeal to lightning (as a normal phenomenon) is typical of wisdom, as is the structure of the correlative. The description of the days of Noah is both an appeal to experience and a prophetic technique of reference to the everyday aspects of life as a sign of what is truly real for the people involved. The parable-like saying in 17:35 simply says that one will be saved, another doomed, when the end comes. This verse thus emphasizes as well the unexpected coming of the end—its arrival is assured, only the time schedule is unknown.

The enigmatic sentence about the eagles clearly demonstrates the versatility of the sentence as a vehicle for both gnomic and eschatological wisdom and the fact that such a distinction can only be clearly made when the context affords an answer.

#47 PARABLE OF POUNDS

Mt. 25:14–30

(14) "For it will be as when a man going on a journey called his servants and entrusted to them his property; (15) to one he gave five talents, to another two, to another one, to each according to his ability. Then he went away. (16) He who had received the five talents went at once and traded with them; and he made five talents more. (17) So too,

Lk. 19:11–27

(11) As they heard these things, he proceeded to tell a parable, because he was near to Jerusalem, and because they supposed that the kingdom of God was to appear immediately. (12) He said therefore, "A nobleman went into a far country to receive kingly power and then return. (13) Calling ten of his servants, he gave them ten pounds,

[8]See above in Chapter III.

he who had the two talents made two talents more. (18) But he who had received the one talent went and dug in the ground and hid his master's money. (19) Now after a long time the master of those servants came and settled accounts with them. (20) And he who had received the five talents came forward, bringing five talents more, saying, 'Master, you delivered to me five talents; here I have made five talents more.' (21) His master said to him, 'Well done, good and faithful servant; you have been faithful over a little, I will set you over much; enter into the joy of your master.' (22) And he also who had the two talents came forward, saying, 'Master, you delivered to me two talents; here I have made two talents more.' (23) His master said to him, 'Well done, good and faithful servant; you have been faithful over a little, I will set you over much; enter into the joy of your master.' (24) He also had received the one talent came forward, saying, 'Master, I knew you to be a hard man, reaping where you did not sow, and gathering where you did not winnow; (25) so I was afraid, and I went and hid your talent in the ground. Here you have what is yours. (26) But his master answered him, 'You wicked and slothful servant! You knew that I reap where I have not sowed, and gather where I have not winnowed? (27) Then you ought to have invested my money with the bankers, and at my coming I should have received what was my own with interest. (28) So take the talent from him, and give it to him who has the ten talents. (29) For to every one who has will more be given, and he will have abundance; but from him who has not, even what he has will be taken away. (30) And cast the worthless servant into the outer darkness; there men will weep and gnash their teeth.' "

and said to them, 'Trade with these till I come.' (14) But his citizens hated him and sent an embassy after him, saying, 'We do not want this man to reign over us.' (15) When he returned, having received the kingly power, he commanded these servants, to whom he had given the money, to be called to him, that he might know what they had gained by trading. (16) The first came before him, saying, 'Lord, your pound has made ten pounds more.' (17) And he said to him, 'Well done, good servant! Because you have been faithful in a very little, you shall have authority over ten cities.' (18) And the second came, saying, 'Lord, your pound has made five pounds. (19) And he said to him, 'And you are to be over five cities.' (20) Then another came, saying, 'Lord, here is your pound, which I kept laid away in a napkin; (21) for I was afraid of you, because you are a severe man; you take up what you did not lay down, and reap what you did not sow.' (22) He said to him, 'I will condemn you out of your own mouth, you wicked servant! You knew that I was a severe man, taking up what I did not lay down and reaping what I did not sow? (23) Why then did you not put my money into the bank, and at my coming I should have collected it with interest?' (24) And he said to those who stood by, 'Take the pound from him, and give it to him who has the ten pounds.' (25) (And they said to him, 'Lord, he has ten pounds!') (26) 'I tell you, that to every one who has will more be given; but from him who has not, even what he has will be taken away. (27) But as for these enemies of mine, who did not want me to reign over them, bring them here and slay them before me.' "

Matthew and Luke have clearly modified a parable to suit their own purposes. The similarities are enough, however, to posit a common tradition. The repeated agreement in the use of the title "Lord" is significant. However, it is only at the end of the pericope that there is enough sequential agreement to allow any precise comparison of form (other than the fact that a parable about a variety of responses to an absent lord does exist as background).

The criticism of the "evil servant" (Lk. 19:22–23) begins in both Gospels with "you knew that" and is followed by a series of examples of the demanding standards of the lord. Thus, the conclusion of the parable is anticipated by an appeal to what the servant already knows—which should have been a clear guide to his action prior to the return of the lord, when the "judgment" will take place.

The conclusion (19:24), very similar again to the style of the apophthegm, is a pronouncement (prophetic) by the lord. The servant who does not learn by the past will be completely rejected.

The section ends with a proverbial statement, which Luke introduces with the prophetic introduction ("I tell you"); that "the rich get richer and the poor get poorer" is assumed to be common wisdom. In this context, however, it becomes an eschatological judgment upon those who have had the opportunity to respond and who have rejected Jesus. If you do not use what you have and what you know, especially when you already know what the principles of judgment will be, you will be condemned.

#48 PRECEDENCE

Mt. 19:28	*Mk. 10:41–45*	*Lk. 22:28–30*
(28) Jesus said to them, "Truly, I say to you, in the new world, when the Son of man shall sit on his glorious throne, you who have followed me will also sit on twelve thrones, judging the twelve tribes of Israel."	(41) And when the ten heard it, they began to be indignant at James and John. (42) And Jesus called them to him and said to them, "You know that those who are supposed to rule over the Gentiles lord it over them, and their great men exercise authority over them. (43) But it shall not be so among you; but	(28) "You are those who have continued with me in my trial; (29) as my Father appointed a kingdom for me, so do I appoint for you (30) that you may eat and drink at my table in my kingdom, and sit on thrones judging the twelve tribes of Israel."

whoever would be great
among you must be your
servant, (44) and whoever
would be first among you
must be a slave of all. (45)
For the Son of man also
came not to be served but
to serve, and to give his life
as a ransom for many."

It is quite likely that the small amount of common material here, and its varied placement by Matthew and Luke, is the result of an isolated saying being attached by catchwords to two quite different contexts.

The combination of throne and judging is consistent with the references to YHWH's judging activity in other levels of tradition. The imputing of judgmental activity to the apostles is unique although the judgment against Israel is, as we have seen, a common factor in the Q community's attitude toward the Jews.

VII

CONCLUSIONS
AND SUGGESTIONS

The peculiar problems of the materials available to us dictated a method which required a series of thematic and form-critical studies and, in turn, a shifting of perspective in order to emphasize specific issues. The fact that there is an eschatological, prophetic, and wisdom tendency embedded within the material could only be demonstrated by actually testing the claim against the text. Since this wisdom dimension had not been generally recognized before, particularly the nonspeculative or aphoristic variety of wisdom, it was necessary to proceed step-by-step. Now that the individual elements of the proposal have been presented, a summary is necessary and the consequences of such an overall outlook must also be faced.

It has been assumed from the start that, if the Q material does come from a self-sustaining group within earliest Christianity, then the attitudes and outlooks of such a community will form a consistent, cohering entity. This circular argument is unavoidable in the interpretation of any written material—the basis for the interpretation must come from a hypothesis suggested by the specifics in the document and can only be confirmed by reference to the material itself.[1] However, the claim for probability (above and beyond mere possibility) is convincing if it can be shown that (1) the environment or cultural context is one in which such an aggregate of ideas and sayings would be comprehensible and that (2) the material itself

1. E. D. Hirsch, *Validity in Interpretation*, (New Haven: Yale University Press, 1967), pp. 196–198.

does actually contain the themes and motifs claimed for it. I am assuming that a case has already been made for the second issue. It is the first which demands our attention here.

The initial problem is to show how such a collection of interests and attitudes can be integrated. The classical distinctions between prophet and wise man would make such a combination questionable. Is it possible to view this community as a single entity or must we postulate that in the course of development there has been a combination of two historically distinct sets of material? S. Schulz has recently argued the latter point. He claims that there are signs of two stages of development in the Q material (he refers to them as older and younger) which account for the specific final concatenation. His proposal, although full of insight at many points, is basically too complex and unnecessary. It assumes that a strict definition of Palestinian and Hellenistic characteristics is possible which will enable the scholar to make detailed, definite judgments about individual pericopes.[2] Rather than speculate about levels of tradition in Q when we do not have a manuscript of Q, it seems preferable to maintain the redaction-critical method of attempting to locate the theology of the latest editor or collector who considered the material to be a sensible collection.

Since there appears to be a variety of interwoven material, can it really be understood as a coherent unity? What first appears as a contradiction—the combining of an imminent eschatology with wisdom forms—can, however, be understood as a sensible theological point of view. The expectation of the imminent return of Jesus to effect the judgment of YHWH leads to a heightened, intense interest in the present time and its circumstances. The past and the future both contribute to the intensification of the awareness of the importance of the present. Every action of an individual in the time just prior to the end—when the end, in a sense, has already begun—takes on an ultimate significance at such a time because it operates within

---

2. Siegfried Schulz, *Q, Die Spruchquelle der Evangelisten* (Zürich: Theologischer Verlag, 1972). This massive analysis of the Q material will demand careful study in the future. Its extensive compilation of data makes it invaluable. However, Schulz's main contribution—the distinction between two layers of tradition—attempts to draw lines which I think are not only questionable but unnecessary. Nevertheless, this book is certain to be a major factor in any discussion of Q for years to come.

an eternal, timeless order where the continuity of action and reaction does not vary in essentials from time-to-time or place-to-place. It assumes that there are certain basic principles which operate above and beyond the control of man. Thus, man's task is to recognize these principles and to act in accordance with them. The difference between conventional wisdom and the eschatological form of wisdom which we see here in Q is that the recognition of basic principles is not merely the result of reflection upon past experience but also because YHWH has acted in the present to warn and encourage those who will listen. The end will soon be here and it is not a time which is continuous with the past; new factors must be considered. Thus, prophecy—whether the words of Jesus or of his inspired followers —informs people of the demands of the present and of the life that is required if they are successfully to survive the judgment.

Prophecy and wisdom are not so distinct as had been assumed. The inclination among Old Testament scholars to acknowledge the presence of wisdom forms and interests in prophetic materials has already been mentioned.[3] Although there is a recognizable order in this world according to late wisdom books, YHWH can and does intervene and overrule that order. Therefore, YHWH's action is an item of experience which must be integrated into one's understanding of the world along side "secular" experience, if experience is a true reflection of the full realities of life. In this sense, the right time for an activity (a prominent theme in wisdom) is compatible with an eschatological approach to life. Those who discern the signs of the times are those who have seen the relationship between a variety of experiences. Apocalyptic is then one variation of the fusing of prophecy and wisdom.

In the previous chapters it has been argued that the Q community has the following characteristics:

an anticipation of the imminent return of Jesus as the Son of Man,

a need to continue to proclaim Jesus' sayings,

a recognition that Jesus is still active within the community by inspiring prophets to speak in his name,

---

3. Cf. the reference to Wolff's work on Amos in Chapter IV.

a need to prepare for his coming by fulfilling the demands placed upon them by the coming judge,

a consciousness of the negative reaction (persecution) toward those who speak and act as Jesus directs them.

As many commentators have pointed out, there is a surprising lack of interest in the saving significance of Jesus' death. If we begin with the assumption that all early theological activity is based upon the so-called *kerygma* (as defined by C. D. Dodd), we would be forced to agree with Dibelius and others that Q is therefore the result of the church's attempt to teach and enlighten those who have already responded favorably to the *kerygma*.[4] In this case, Q is classified as *didache*, i.e., as teaching; there must have been a prior proclamation and, if it is not presented in Q, it must already be known by those who are addressed.

Such a monolithic understanding of early Christian theology is in error. There are numerous indications that a variety of responses to Jesus existed in the years following his death.[5] It is the thesis of this study that Q preserves such a non-*kerygmatic* approach. Salvation is promised to those who respond to Jesus as the Son of Man and who are prepared for his imminent return. The death of Jesus is understood as a feature of the last days before the coming of the Kingdom when the forces of evil attempt to destroy those who speak in YHWH's name. The fate of the prophets has always been persecution, misunderstanding, and often death; as Jesus died at the hands of those who claim to be God's people, so those who follow in his steps can expect persecution. His death is highly significant, but it is not the basis of salvation.

Tödt has already pointed to the lack of Old Testament passages in Q which refer to the saving nature of Jesus' death.[6] There is an implicit assumption in Q that Jesus is alive and a source of inspiration, although there is no speculation about, or recounting of, the

---

4. Cf. the discussion above in Chapter II.
5. Walter Bauer, *Orthodoxy and Heresy in Earliest Christianity* (Philadelphia: Fortress press, 1971) and J. M. Robinson and H. Koester, *Trajectories through Early Christianity* (Philadelphia: Fortress Press, 1971).
6. H. E. Tödt, *The Son of Man in the Synoptic Tradition* (Philadelphia: Westminster Press, 1965), pp. 266–269.

resurrection. Rather, the emphasis is placed upon the practical necessities of the end-time—one must prepare for the coming of the Kingdom and its attendant judgment. The judge was here among us and is soon to come. In a similar vein, there is also a noticeable absence of apocalyptic speculation. Rather than speculate about the course of events during the last days, the Q community has preserved the wisdom of the Son of Man—either spoken directly by him or spoken by his prophets.

The significance of the large number of wisdom forms must be considered as a determinative indication of this community's understanding of their situation. Their approach is a practical one—to prepare for the coming. They consider Jesus to be a combination of teacher, prophet, and wise man. His advice for the future is crucial and should be understood as an integral part of the basic experience of men in a world which is about to reach its climax. His teaching breaks certain conventional categories but is not presented as a new, radical assertion. Rather, it is a new way of looking at YHWH's demands because of the imminence of the Kingdom.

Thus, a combination of wisdom, eschatology, and prophecy is possible and sensible in the days prior to 70 A.D. It is impossible to locate such a community with any precision, but the use of Greek and the lack of influence from Pauline thought would tend to indicate Northern Palestine or Syria during the forties.

The fact that Matthew and Luke do incorporate the Q material in their Gospels indicates that a conflation of early "theologies" is taking place after 70. It is not possible to decide whether Mark knew any Q material because of our reliance on literary-critical methods to define the extent of Q. However, Mark has put into a narrative form the basic thought of the Pauline school. Jesus died for our sins and we are forgiven by God because of his death (within an apocalyptic framework). When Matthew and Luke expand the Markan material, they incorporate a greater number of sayings and construct a different message without giving up Mark's basic theme about the suffering of the Son of Man. It is the redactional activity of Matthew and Luke which contributes to our inability to reconstruct the order of Q. However, it is clear that these later evangelists are attempting to accommodate the Q material, and its theology, into their basic

Markan point of view. More extensive work needs to be done on this problem of the use of Q by Matthew and Luke and is not appropriate here. However, the main point is clear: Matthew and Luke, although they have preserved Q for us, do not share the Q theology but rather wish to incorporate the sayings of Jesus within a narrative about his life.[7]

As a result of this situation, we can get a fairly clear idea of the relationship among these early theologies. Q is quite distinct. But it is a theology which does not survive the syncretistic activity of the post-Pauline church. The orthodox point of view (i.e., the understanding of Christianity which gains dominance) emerges as a combination of emphases which, if seen independently, would undoubtedly be declared heretical. Robinson's suggestion that a sayings tradition was developed later into Gnostic form, and appeared eventually as the Gospel of Thomas, would explain how other "Christians" are making use of earlier traditions. The following chart may help to clarify the possibilities:

Early Responses
to Jesus   c.70   c.80–95

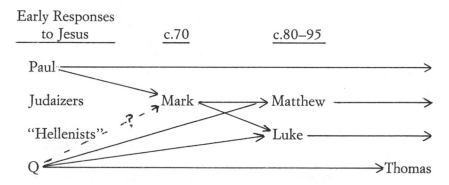

This is only a sketch, of course. Nevertheless, it does account for the way in which Q is preserved and why there are no remaining Q manuscripts. Because of the development toward orthodoxy and the emphasis on apostolic authority in the later decades of the first century, the variety of early responses to Jesus has been suppressed.

---

7. Cf. especially Norman Perrin, *The New Testament: An Introduction* (New York: Harcourt, Brace, Jovanovich, 1974), pp. 175–177, 200–205 and the references cited there.

The "orthodox solution" has found a way of combining theologies which do not necessarily conflict but which are definitely distinct at their time of origin.

As an example of an early tradition which is used by a later evangelist, the analysis of Acts 3 by Zehnle is instructive.[8] He suggests that Luke draws upon a source which he finds useful, but which is not typical of the full-blown theology of the third evangelist. Acts 2 shows definite signs of Lukan redaction from both emendation *and* composition analysis. However, in Acts 3 there are themes and concepts with which Luke is sympathetic but which he has not completely rewritten. That is, Acts 3 appears to be composed of elements from an older tradition which have not been fully reworked by Luke.

This possibility, in itself, is an important indication of the way Luke composes his two-volume story. But, beyond this, Zehnle points to certain features of Acts 3 which are parallel to the emphases we have highlighted as a part of Q. The most significant is Christology. The importance of Jesus lies in his preaching of repentance and his attempt to prepare the people for the coming of the messianic times. He is the prophet who was foretold by Moses and who was persecuted by the people because of their ignorance. Jesus is the messiah but his role is not delineated (unlike the Son of Man emphasis in Q). He is the eschatological prophet whose message must be continually proclaimed while he is in heaven awaiting the final act of God.

The importance of Zehnle's study of Acts 2 and 3 in relation to Q is twofold: (1) an early tradition probably lies behind the speech in Acts 3 and suggests the existence of an ancient theology which Luke incorporates into his account and (2) the nature of this ancient tradition shows some close similarity to the self-understanding of Q as we have defined it. Whether they are one and the same, it is not possible to say—primarily because the extent of Lukan redaction cannot be precisely known (on Q and on Acts 3). Nevertheless, the existence of an early non-Pauline theology similar to Q seems likely.

The details of a wisdom-based style of thinking have been emphasized in this study because it has not been given full consideration

8. Richard F. Zehnle, *Peter's Pentecost Discourse,* SBL Monograph no. 15 (Nashville: Abingdon Press, 1971).

previously. But this fact raises the question, why is such an issue being considered now? Certainly part of the answer lies in the fact that there is a general renaissance today of the study of wisdom literature which has made many scholars more alert to such tendencies in the Q material. For example, Walter Brueggemann has recently described wisdom as the neglected side of biblical faith.[9]

In the wake of the theological character of neo-orthodoxy with its concern about the distinction between proclamation (*kerygma*) and teaching (parenesis or *didache*), the experience-based, world-oriented approach which wisdom represents was considered peripheral if not simply heretical. However, as the tenor of theological thought shifted more recently to a more positive attitude toward secularity, and with existentialism's positive evaluation of the human dimension in religious experience, the positive attitude toward the world which is typical of wisdom literature has become more and more a matter of interest to biblical scholars.

This situation is indicative not only of the fact that there are trends which develop in biblical studies as well as in other disciplines, but also of the general hermeneutical principle that the cultural context determines the way in which one is able to interpret a text.

In this light, there are some suggestions to be made about the significance of Q as it has been presented here. These thoughts are far from complete and are intended only as indications of the wider impact the historical study might have.

First of all, the basic thrust of the theology of hope has been to replace an emphasis upon the past with a stress upon looking toward the future for a way of understanding man and his place in the world.[10] It is the interaction of one's understanding of the past, present, and future which has been rethought by this school of theology. It suggests that we must build upon the past not only in the sense of knowing where we have come from; we need to discover consciously a way of moving from the present into the future. In a way, one might argue that the past *and* the future both contribute to

9. Walter Brueggemann, *In Man We Trust: The Neglected Side of Biblical Faith* (Richmond: John Knox Press, 1972).
10. Jürgen Moltmann, *Theology of Hope* (New York: Harper & Row, 1967) and Walter H. Capps, *Time Invades the Cathedral* (Philadelphia: Fortress Press, 1972).

an understanding of the present. Because we have been too history-oriented, we have failed to see the reality of the future and the significance it has in molding our self-understanding.

The interpretation of Q presented in the preceding chapters could serve as an illustration of such a future-based program. Because the future is so real, this Q community is virtually standing on its tiptoes in anticipation of the parousia. Without ignoring the past it is nonetheless free from the tyranny of history. History helps to inform the present by supplying guidelines for interpretation. But history is not the central factor in determining a way of life. For experience, in its everyday sensibility, and informed by the sayings of the judge, is the key to developing a way of life which will lead to a positive future.

Secondly, even though it is a future-oriented community, the material world is not ignored. There is a tendency within Christianity to "spiritualize" or rarify any forward-looking theology to the point where the world and material things are simply not relevant to its concerns. This is definitely not the case for the Q community. The clan wisdom traditions are indicative of a healthy acknowledgment of the importance of life and its context within the basic religious outlook. With its emphasis on the secular, we can learn from the Q community how it is possible to be both religious and secular, with a positive attitude toward worldly experience.

Of course, the prophetic element should warn us that this is a world not of our own making—that God does speak through his prophets as through the Son of Man.

Thirdly, the theology of hope has emphasized the corporate and social dimensions of the faith and this is also present in Q. Each individual is responsible for his actions, but it is man in the context of the community where real learning and action takes place. Each individual must be aware of his relationship to others in the variety of communities in which he lives.

Finally, hope is action—not talk about hope; the essence of the theology of Q is not speculation, explanation, or exposition, but the presentation of the message—i.e., placing the demands and the new situation before people and encouraging them to act in such a way that they will be able to survive at the time of the arrival of the Kingdom.

The general cultural context of our world and that of Q appear to be quite similar. Both times are apocalyptic—when we anticipate a time which will be "new" but which is dependent on the past. We use the past not as a model but as an indication of what can happen and how bad it has been. Science fiction and related fantasy books continue to be popular—not merely because they are escape literature, but because the future, not the past, holds our attention and our hopes. The future is not just "out there"; it is increasingly decisive in helping to determine how we will act toward other human beings and the environment.

Bibliography
and
Indexes

A SELECT
BIBLIOGRAPHY ON Q

No bibliography can ever be complete. There are many books which could have been included, such as introductions to the New Testament or the Synoptic Problem, commentaries on Matthew or Luke, studies of individual pericopes or words, etc. This particular list contains those books and articles which are either (1) most relevant to the discussion of the theology of Q or (2) which deal directly with the problem of Q in one form or another. It is a good place to begin.

Argyle, A. W. "The Accounts of the Temptation of Jesus in Relation to the Q Hypothesis." *Expository Times* 64 (1952/53):382.

Bacon, B. W. "The Nature and Design of Q, the Second Synoptic Source." *Hibbert Journal* 22 (1923/24): 674–688.

Bammel, E. "Das Ende von Q." *Verborum veritas*. Festschrift for G. Stahlin. Wuppertal, 1970, pp. 39–50.

Barrett, C. K. "Q: A Re-examination." *Expository Times* 54 (1942/43): 320–323.

Beardslee, William A. *Literary Criticism of the New Testament.* Guides to Biblical Scholarship. Philadelphia: Fortress Press, 1970.

———. "The Motif of Fulfillment in the Eschatology of the Synoptic Gospels." In *Transitions in Biblical Scholarship,* edited by J. C. Rylaarsdam. Chicago: University of Chicago Press, 1968, pp. 171–191.

———."The Wisdom Tradition and the Synoptic Gospels." *Journal of the American Academy of Religion* 35 (1967):231–240.

Brown, J. P. "The Form of 'Q' Known to Matthew." *New Testament Studies* 8 (1961/62):27–42.

————. "Mark as Witness to an Edited Form of Q." *Journal of Biblical Literature* 80 (1961):29–44.

Bultmann, Rudolf. *History of the Synoptic Tradition,* trans. John Marsh from the 3d German ed. Oxford: Basil Blackwell, and New York: Harper & Row, 1963.

Bussby, F. "Is Q an Aramaic Document?" *Expository Times* 65 (1953/54): 272–275.

Bussmann, W. "Hat es nie eine schriftliche Logienquelle gegeben?" *Zeitschrift für die neutestamentliche Wissenschaft* 31 (1932):23–32.

Butler, B. C. *The Originality of St. Matthew. A Critique of the Two-Document Hypothesis.* Cambridge: Cambridge University Press, 1951.

Carlston, C. and Norlin, D. "Once More—Statistics and Q." *Harvard Theological Review* 64 (1971):59–78.

Castor, G. D. "The Relation of Mark to the Source Q." *Journal of Biblical Literature* 31 (1912):82–91.

Crum, J. M. C. "Mark and 'Q.' " *Theology* 12 (1926):275–282.

————. *The Original Jerusalem Gospel. Being Essays on the Document Q.* London: Constable & Co., 1927.

Curtis, K. P. G. "In Support of Q." *Expository Times* 84 (1973):309–310.

Danner, Dan. "The Q Document and the Words of Jesus." Unpublished paper.

Davies, W. D. *The Setting of the Sermon on the Mount.* Cambridge: Cambridge University Press, 1964.

Devisch, M. "Le document Q, source de Matthieu: Problématique actuelle." In Didier, M., *L'Évangile selon Matthieu: Rédaction et théologie.* Bibliotheca Ephemeridum Theologicarum Lovaniensium 29. Gembloux: J. Duculot, 1972, pp. 71–98.

Dibelius, Martin. *From Tradition to Gospel,* trans. in collaboration with the author by Bertram Lee Woolf from the rev. 2d German ed. London: Nicholson and Watson, 1934, and New York: Charles Scribner's Sons, 1935.

Downing, F. G. "Toward the Rehabilitation of Q." *New Testament Studies* 11 (1964/65):169–181.

Dungan, D. L. "Mark—The Abridgment of Matthew and Luke." In *Jesus and Man's Hope.* Vol. I. Pittsburgh: Pittsburgh Theological Seminary, 1970.

Edwards, R. A. "An Approach to a Theology of Q." *Journal of Religion* 51 (1971):247–269.

————. *A Concordance to Q.* Missoula, Montana: Scholars Press, 1975 [Greek text].

————. "The Eschatological Correlative as a *Gattung* in the New Testament," *Zeitschrift für die neutestamentliche Wissenschaft* 60 (1969): 9–20.

————. *The Sign of Jonah in the Theology of the Evangelists and Q.* Studies in Biblical Theology, #18 Second Series. London: SCM Press, 1971.

Farmer, W. R. *The Synoptic Problem. A Critical Analysis.* New York: Macmillan, 1964.

Farrer, A. M. "On Dispensing with Q." In *Studies in the Gospels; Essays in Memory of R. H. Lightfoot,* edited by D. E. Nineham. Oxford: Basil Blackwell, 1957, pp. 55–88.

Fitzmyer, Joseph A., S.J. "The Priority of Mark and the 'Q' Source in Luke." In *Jesus and Man's Hope.* Vol. I. Pittsburgh: Pittsburgh Theological Seminary, 1970, pp. 131–170.

Gilbert, C. H. "The Jesus of Q—The Oldest Synoptic Source." *Hibbert Journal* 10 (1911/12):533–542.

Haenchen, E. "Matthäus 23." *Zeitschrift für Theologie und Kirche* 48 (1951):38–63.

Harnack, Adolf von. *The Sayings of Jesus.* London: Williams & Norgate and New York: G. P. Putnam's Sons, 1908.

Hawkins, John C. *Horae Synopticae.* Oxford: Clarendon Press, 1909.

————. "Probabilities as to the so-called Double Tradition of St. Matthew and St. Luke." In *Studies in the Synoptic Problem.* Oxford: Clarendon Press, 1911.

Hoffman, Paul. "Die Anfänge der Theologie in der Logienquelle." In J. Schreiner-G. Dautzenberg, *Gestalt und Anspruch des Neuen Testaments.* Wurzburg, 1969, pp. 134–152.

————. "Jesusverkündigung in der Logienquelle." In *Jesus in den Evangelien* (SBS 45). Stuttgart, 1970, pp. 50–70.

————. *Studien zur Theologie der Logienquelle* NTAbh, n.f. 8. Münster: Aschendorff, 1972.

————. "Die Versuchungsgeschichte in der Logienquelle." *Biblische Zeitschrift* 13 (1969):207–223.

Honey, T. E. "Did Mark Use Q?" *Journal of Biblical Literature* 62 (1943):319–331.

Jeremias, J. "Zur Hypothese einer schriftlichen Logienquelle Q." *Zeitschrift für die neutestamentliche Wissenschaft* 29 (1930):147 ff.

Käsemann, Ernst. "The Beginnings of Christian Theology." In *New Testament Questions of Today,* trans. W. J. Montague. London: SCM Press, and Philadelphia: Fortress Press, 1969, pp. 82–107.

————. "Sentences of Holy Law in the New Testament." In *New Testament Questions of Today,* trans. W. J. Montague. London: SCM Press, and Philadelphia: Fortress Press, 1969, pp. 66–81.

————. "On the Subject of Primitive Christian Apocalyptic." In *New Testament Questions of Today*, trans. W. J. Montague. London: SCM Press, and Philadelphia: Fortress Press, 1969, pp. 108–138.

Kee, Howard. *Jesus in History*. New York: Harcourt, Brace & World, Inc., 1970.

Kilpatrick, G. D. "The Disappearance of Q." *Journal of Theological Studies* 42 (1941):184.

Koester, H. "One Jesus and Four Primitive Gospels," *Harvard Theological Review* 61 (1968):203–247; also in *Trajectories through Early Christianity*, edited by J. M. Robinson and H. Koester. Philadelphia: Fortress Press, 1971, pp. 158–204.

Lake, K. "The Date of Q." *The Expositor* 7 (1909):494–507.

Leon-Dufour, X. "Redaktionsgeschichte of Matthew and Literary Criticism." In *Jesus and Man's Hope*. Vol. I. Pittsburgh: Pittsburgh Theological Seminary, 1970.

Linton, Olof. "The Q Problem Reconsidered." In *Studies in New Testament and Early Christian Literature; Essays in Honor of Allen P. Wikgren*, edited by D. E. Aune. Leiden: E. J. Brill, 1972, pp. 43–59.

Lührmann, D. *Die Redaktion der Logienquelle*. WMANT 33. Neukirchen-Vluyn: Neukirchener Verlag, 1969.

Lummis, E. "A Case Against Q." *Hibbert Journal* 24 (1925/26):764.

Luz, U. "Die wiederentdeckte Logienquelle." *Evangelische Theologie* 33 (1973):527–533.

Manson, T. W. *The Sayings of Jesus*. London: SCM Press, 1937; also appeared as part of *The Mission and Message of Jesus*, edited by Major, H. D. A., Manson, T. W., and Wright, C. J. New York: E. P. Dutton & Co., 1938.

————. *The Teaching of Jesus*. Cambridge: Cambridge University Press, 1963.

Mees, Michael. "Zur Frage der Logienquelle." *Theologie der Gegenwart in Auswahl* 14 (1971):103–106.

Meyer, Paul D. "The Community of Q." Ph.D. dissertation. University of Iowa, 1967.

Moffatt, James. *An Introduction to the Literature of the New Testament* 3d rev. ed., 1918. Edinburgh: T. & T. Clark, 1961.

North, R. "Chenoboskion and Q." *Catholic Biblical Quarterly* 24 (1962): 154–170.

Patton, C. S. "Did Mark Use Q? Or Did Q Use Mark?" *American Journal of Theology* 16 (1912):634–642.

Perrin, N. *The New Testament: An Introduction*. New York: Harcourt, Brace, Jovanovich, Inc., 1974.

Petrie, Stewart, " 'Q' is only what you make it." *Novum Testamentum* 3 (1959):28–33.

Pokorny, Petr. "The Temptation Stories and Their Intention." *New Testament Studies* 20 (1974): 115–127.

———. "Die Worte Jesu nach der Logienquelle in Lichte des zeitgenössischen Judentums." *Kairos* 11 (1969):172–180.

Polag, A. "Die Christologie der Logienquelle." Unpublished dissertation. Treves, 1968.

———. "Zu den Stufen der Christologie in Q." *Studia Evangelica* 4 (Texte und Untersuchungen 102). Berlin, 1968.

———."Der Umfang der Logienquelle." Unpublished dissertation. Treves, 1966.

Robinson, James M. "Basic Shifts in German Theology." *Interpretation* 16 (1962):76–97.

———. "Jesus as Sophos and Sophia, Wisdom Tradition and the Gospels." Unpublished paper read at Notre Dame, 1973.

———. "Logoi Sophon: On the Gattung of Q." In *Trajectories through Early Christianity,* edited by James M. Robinson and H. Koester. Philadelphia: Fortress Press, 1971, pp. 71–113.

Rosché, T. "The Words of Jesus and the Future of the Q Hypothesis." *Journal of Biblical Literature* 79 (1960):210–220.

Sanders, E. P. "The Argument from Order and the Relationship between Matthew and Luke." *New Testament Studies* 15 (1968/69):249–261.

———. "The Overlaps of Mark and Q and the Synoptic Problem." *New Testament Studies* 19 (1972/73):453–465.

———. *The Tendencies of the Synoptic Tradition* (Society for New Testament Studies. Monograph Series, 9). Cambridge: Cambridge University Press, 1969.

Schmithals, Walter. "Kein Streit um des Kaisers Bart: Zur Diskussion über das Bekenntnis zu Jesus Christus." *Evangelische Kommentare* 3 (1970):76–82.

Schulz, S. *Q, Die Spruchquelle der Evangelisten.* Zürich: Theologischer Verlag, 1972.

Stanton, G. N. "On the Christology of Q." In *Christ and Spirit in the New Testament* edited by Linders, B., and Smalley, S. Cambridge: Cambridge University Press, 1973, pp. 27–42.

Steck, O. H. *Israel und das gewaltsame Geschick der Propheten.* WMANT 23. Neukirchen-Vluyn: Neukirchener Verlag, 1967.

Streeter, B. H. *The Four Gospels: A Study of Origins.* London: Macmillan, 1926.

———. "St. Mark's Knowledge and Use of Q." In *Studies in the Synoptic Problem,* Members of the University of Oxford, edited by W. Sanday. Oxford: Clarendon Press, 1911, pp. 165–183.

Suggs, M. J. *Wisdom, Christology, and Law in Matthew's Gospel.* Cambridge: Harvard University Press, 1970.

Taylor, V. "The Elusive Q." *Expository Times* 46 (1934/35):68–74.
————. "The Order of Q." *Journal of Theological Studies* 4 (1953): 27–31.
————. "The Original Order of Q." In *New Testament Essays: Studies in Memory of T. W. Manson,* edited by A. J. Higgins. Manchester: University of Manchester Press, 1959, pp. 246–269.
Throckmorton, Burton H. "Did Mark know Q?" *Journal of Biblical Literature* 67 (1948):319–339.
Tödt, Heinz Eduard. *The Son of Man in the Synoptic Tradition,* trans. Dorothea M. Barton. Philadelphia: Westminster Press, 1965.
Turner, Nigel. "Q in Recent Thought." *Expository Times* 80 (1969): 324–328.
Vögtle, Anton. "Der Spruch vom Jonaszeichen." In *Synoptische Studien: Alfred Wilkenhauser zum siebzigsten Geburtstag am 22. Februar 1593 dargebracht von Freunden, Kollegen und Schulern.* München: Karl Zink Verlag, 1953, pp. 230–277.
Worden, Ronald D. "A Philological Analysis of Luke 6:20b–49 and Parallels." Ph.D. dissertation. Princeton Seminary, 1973.
Wrege, H.-Th. *Die Überlieferungsgeschichte der Bergpredigt.* WUNT 9. Tübingen, 1968.

INDEXES

1 Corinthians
1:20 — 136

1 Thessalonians
4:13–5:11 — 43

INDEX OF AUTHORS